Bits &
Pieces

Bits & Pieces

A Collection of Writing on Grief and Hope

LINDSEY HOLT

XULON PRESS

Xulon Press
2301 Lucien Way #415
Maitland, FL 32751
407.339.4217
www.xulonpress.com

Keep up with Lindsey's latest publications and reach out for inquiries through her website:https://lindseyholt7.wixsite.com/portfolio

Paperback ISBN-13: 978-1-6628-1485-3

DEDICATION

For Lauren and Anabel:
Thank you for being my glimpse of heaven on earth.
I love you, and I'm counting down the moments.

TABLE OF CONTENTS

Lauren & Lindsey

Lauren, Anabel, & Lindsey

Lindsey & Anabel

FOREWORD

EIGHTEEN AND TWENTY-TWO.

My world has crumbled twice: first at age eighteen, then at age twenty-two. When I was eighteen, one of my best friends, Anabel, passed away in a bus accident. Four years later (to the very month) I lost my sister, Lauren, in a car accident.

Needless to say, I now have massive amounts of travel anxiety.

After losing Anabel, I talked about her a lot. I felt the need to keep her with me in my everyday life and conversation. I wanted to honor her memory and carry on her legacy. I was very public about what she meant to me. After losing Lauren, I turned inward with my grief. I knew parts of my grief journey would be the same, but parts of it would be vastly different. This second loss felt so private to me, so devastating to my core, that I felt as if my very DNA had been altered. I didn't know how to talk about this one. I didn't know how to carry on this time.

So, I began to write. I wrote and I wrote, and I put all the thoughts I wasn't sure how to say out loud onto paper. I wrote about my anguish and my confusion and my questions. I wrote about glimpses of hope that I caught, and I wrote about the wonder I felt as God met me in my grief, revealing himself to me again and again. I wrote from a perspective of raw, fresh grief, and I wrote from a perspective of calmer, seasoned grief. On the days I thought I would positively burst from my need to talk to my sister, I sat down and wrote her letters. I wrote prayers and poems and made bullet point lists to organize my tangled thoughts. I kept scraps of paper where I jotted down thoughts as they came to me. There were big, long stretches of time where the words just wouldn't come at all, and then there were moments when I couldn't get the words out fast enough.

Most of all, I wrote because I wanted to remember. I wanted to remember every tiny little thing about Anabel and Lauren. I wanted to remember the lessons God was teaching me. I wanted to remember the things that were helpful to me, and I wanted to remember the things I should never say to a grieving person. I wanted to be able to look back and see that God was working in my heart and in my life all along. I wanted to establish standing stones along the road so that I could turn back on the days I could not see the way forward and know that God has always been and always will be with me.

Five years later, I found myself with this collection of bits and pieces. In many ways, I know my grief journey is still just beginning. I still have so much to learn, but this felt like a good time to gather my thoughts and my words into one place.

There are a few names you might need to know as you read through this book. Lauren and Anabel I have already mentioned. Then there's Heath, who is my husband. He was my high school sweetheart, and we ran around in our church youth group together with Anabel and a few other very dear friends. There's Trent, who was Lauren's husband. They met in the LCU Praise Choir and were set up by a mutual family friend. They dated for three years and were married for almost two when the accident happened. Lastly, there's Darcy, our golden retriever, who was a six-month-old puppy at the time of Lauren's accident. If you aren't a dog person, you probably won't get this, but he became an invaluable form of emotional support for me in my grief journey. I have spent many days weeping into his fur, and he has kissed my tears away. He reads my moods and comes to cuddle me when I'm down. He is the angel of comfort I didn't know I was going to need.

Of all the burdens I pictured myself learning to carry in my life, grief was never one of them. I don't imagine it would be on anyone's list. Then, one day, that thing that you thought would never happen to you has happened. It is your loved one's name on the accident report or in the obituary. It is your loved one's face being shared on everyone else's social media. Those sad stories you sometimes hear on the news about someone else have become your devastating reality, and you think to yourself, "What on earth am I going to do now?"

If you need professional counseling and/or grief expertise (which I believe all people do) I am probably (definitely) not the one you need to talk to. But if you just want someone to hold your hand through this journey, I can do that. If you need someone to verbalize the complicated, snarling thoughts of grief, maybe you can relate to something you find in this book. If you need a moment to just sit and acknowledge that grief is terribly hard without having to put a positive spin on it, I can definitely do that. If you are desperate for a glimpse of hope, I hope you will find one here.

You will smile again, dear one, I promise.

Unraveled

When the cord so sweet and strong—so central to my life, so precious to my soul—when that strand broke, the devastation was complete.

I unraveled.

I look around in hopelessness at the bits and pieces which used to be me. The way I used to laugh. The way I used to dream.

Now I just find myself grasping at strings.

I search through the shreds, desperate to find an unbroken strand.

The one I know will hold.

I sift through the broken bits and pieces, the frayed and tangled mess—the things that make me cringe in fear; the way my smile doesn't reach my eyes; the times I have to slip away to somewhere quiet so I can weep—the bits and pieces that don't seem like me yet are somehow the pieces of my reality.

Jumbled, knotted, tangled bits and pieces. Shapeless, formless, useless remnants.

But I search, I hold, I cling to the one unbroken strand as if my life depends on it. And it does.

My very life, my very existence rests on the strength of that one unbroken strand. My bits and pieces blow away and scatter in the winds of my grief. But still, I cling to the strand that was woven deep into my core, the strand that knit me together long before my time began.

Unchanging. Unfailing. Steadfast. Good, true, and holy.

And when my grief makes my bits and pieces crumble further into specks and shreds, I close my eyes and hold fast to that strand.

Because around that cord of truth, the Creator is weaving a tapestry. Scraps of who I was. Strands of who I am becoming. Pieces of those I carry with me. New threads and themes emerging: warm tones of compassion and empathy; cool, calm colors of perspective; and surprisingly bright glimpses of hope. Because even in the mist of the most hopeless unraveling, one cord holds true and faithful.

One strand, one hope, the anchor for my soul.

"We have this hope as an anchor for the soul, firm and secure..." (Heb. 6:19a).

BREATHING

IF YOU'VE EVER EXPERIENCED A CRISIS OR A tragedy, there are certain sights, sounds, and moments which become permanently burned into your memory. All I have to do to recall my own is close my eyes:

My phone rings; there's been a bus accident, but we think everyone is okay; pacing the room; waiting for answers; different stories from different people; lots of fatalities, no fatalities, one fatality; a phone call; worst fears confirmed; knees buckling...

Waking up to the sound of a knock on the bedroom door; there's been an accident—Lauren didn't make it; hearing my grandparents weep when they heard the news; spending Thanksgiving Day planning a funeral; shopping with my mother to pick out a final outfit for my sweet sister; staring at the closed casket that held her; whispering words of love to her...

Even as I write these words, my throat closes up and I struggle to breathe. If you have ever lost someone, you are familiar with this sickening feeling. In the days and hours (and weeks and months and years) that follow the news, there come moments of silence and still-ness—pockets of time when you aren't writing an obit-uary or sorting through pictures for a slideshow—and those moments are the worst. In those times, the horror, the anguish, the despair, the "what ifs," the "what nows," and a million other thoughts come rushing at you and threaten to choke the very life out of you. They crowd in so tightly that you struggle just to draw another breath.

In grief, even the simple task of breathing can be hard.

So, what do you do when you can't breathe? When there are no words, just agonizing pain? How do you pray, how do you think, how do you survive?

I breathe breath prayers.

My college minister taught me about breath prayers years ago. You pick a short phrase, simple words that speak the cries of your heart, and you breathe them: In and out. In and out. My current favorite is this: "Abba Father, have mercy on me." In: "Abba Father." Out: "Have mercy on me." In and out, over and over.

When you close your eyes and can see nothing but horrible memories of your tragedy, when the pain is crippling, when fears and worries about the future start to suffocate you, breathe a breath prayer. Breathing in and out and letting your spirit cry out to God pushes away the terrible thoughts from Satan. Breathing creates room in your mind for the peace and love that is completely impossible to understand. Let that peace and love fill you.

Breathe. Trust. Breathe some more. God is faithful.

SKATING

LAUREN AND I SHARED A LOT OF THINGS growing up. We shared a bathroom, we shared clothes, and we shared the backseat of the car on vacation. When we got older, we shared a cell phone (which meant she always got it because she was older), and we shared a car (which, again, meant she always got it). We shared a sense of humor and we shared our taste in movies and music. We even practically shared a face; people got us confused all the time. You know what else we shared? Skates.

My mom has the best picture of us skating at the park. We were in some sort of awkward, three-legged-race formation, each with a roller skate on our outside foot and holding hands with our skate-less legs in the middle trying to keep our balance. To me, this picture perfectly explains what it is like to grow up with a sister: the hand to hold, the secret keeper, the built-in best friend, the other roller skate.

But what happens when you lose a skate? When you lose the person who held your hand to help you roll along through life? You feel unstable. Lopsided. Out of control. There is never a more obvious need for the other skate than when it is suddenly gone.

For others who were not as close to the person who passed away, the loss will make them stumble, and maybe even trip and fall. But eventually, they get back up and start to skate again because their home base, their foundation, has remained unchanged. But when it is someone you depended upon—your kindred spirit, your spouse, your best friend, your guardian, your sibling, your mentor, your other skate—you cannot ever skate the same.

One of the hardest things about grief is watching the world pick up and move on. Your heart wants to cry out, "How? How are they able to keep going? Don't they know what has been lost?" Many days, I feel hopeless at the thought of trying to pick up and move. I don't know how to operate anymore without my other half. Not only that, I don't *want* to learn how to do without what I have lost. I don't want to ever not need my sister or my best friend.

Unfortunately, never moving again is not an option, nor is it a healthy decision. (However, I will admit, it frequently sounds like a pretty appealing course of inaction to me.) We have to keep skating. We have races left to run. We have a Father who loves us and will give us the strength and courage to keep going. And friends, getting up can take some hefty, heavenly doses of courage.

I will forever skate with a limp, not crippled by my grief, but marked by the love I still carry for those I have lost. Neither Lauren nor I were ever very athletic (my knees were covered in band-aids in the picture) but when I get to heaven, you'd better believe we are going to skate together again. It will be the smoothest, most joy-filled ride I have ever known.

"So do not fear, for I am with you; do not be dismayed, for I am your God. I will strengthen you and help you; I will uphold you with my righteous right hand" (Isaiah 41:10).

Middle School

Do you remember how it felt to be in middle school?

You walk around looking like a perfectly normal (albeit awkward) human being on the outside, but on the inside you have raging turmoil caused by hormones determined to ruin your life.

You feel like you don't fit in your own skin anymore.

There is a new, thin, fragile line between the best day ever and the worst day of your life. You become hyper-aware of other people's words and actions and whether or not they're actually directed toward you.

Maybe the cute boy or girl in your class cracks a joke about something you said. On the outside you laugh, but on the inside you analyze the situation over and over again until you decide switching to home school and/or leaving the country seem to be the most reasonable courses of action.

Take the dramatics down a notch or two (or fifty, if you were an especially angsty preteen) and you'll find that grief is a lot like middle school.

In my grief, I feel like I don't fit in my own skin. I'm not ME anymore; I've been fundamentally changed. For twenty-two years of my life, I never woke up and thought to myself, "I have a sister." I didn't need to. It was just a reality woven into the fabric of my life, one of the characteristics that made me, me. But what happens when reality shifts? When the fabric of your life unravels? I never had to think to myself that I had a sister because it was all I had ever known. But now, I wake up and think to myself, "My sister is gone." That is my new reality.

What was known, guaranteed, and true changed for me in one, earth-shattering moment.

I used to be just Lindsey. Then, I became Lindsey-who-lost-her-best-friend followed by Lindsey-who-lost-her-sister. My "just Lindsey" skin doesn't fit anymore, and with each loss, I struggle to know how to wear my new reality. My life is divided into pre-accident and post-accident, before and after. Before Lindsey was excited, social, energetic, and resilient. After Lindsey is afraid, private, weary, and fragile.

Every day I walk a fine line between a calm, peaceful spirit and the raw, raging feelings of my broken heart. Some days I travel on one side of the line, and some days I find myself on the other. More often than not, I'll spend my days swinging back and forth between the two with no predictability or control. (If the words "no predictability or control" don't sound like middle school emotions to you, I don't know what will.)

There was a time in my life when I thought middle school would be the longest, most dreary years I would ever face. Then, I encountered grief.

I live a lot of days when becoming a hermit or leaving the country to avoid any and all contact with people sounds like a great idea. Unlike middle school, which only lasts 2-3 years, grief is a *lifelong* journey. From where I stand, in the early months and years of this journey, I feel weary just thinking about the days ahead.

I have written and verbalized a lot of my honest feelings over the past few months because I believe that transparency is a huge part of healing, and I want to help others understand how hard and complex grief can be. However, I also want to be sure that people get the chance to hear about the Holy Truth which pierces through the darkness and confusion of grief, the Unfailing Love which serves as an anchor and a foundation in the midst of storms of turmoil and chaos, and the Everlasting Goodness which rights all wrongs.

Feel like your skin doesn't fit anymore? Try this on for size:

> *"Do not fear, for I have redeemed you; I have summoned you by name; you are mine. When you pass through the waters, I will be with you; and when you pass through the rivers, they will not sweep over you. When you walk through the fire, you will not be burned; the flames will not set you ablaze"* (Isa. 43:1b-2).

That earthly skin that does not fit you anymore was never meant to be yours to keep. Your eternal identity lies in the fact that the Creator summons you by name and declares you to be his. The fact that you don't quite fit is just a clear indication of your true identity, and not a single element of this world—not water, not fire, not even *death*—can destroy that reality.

Feeling tossed back and forth by emotions? Find refuge in stillness:

> *"God is our refuge and strength, an ever-present help in trouble. Therefore we will not fear, though the earth give way and the mountains fall into the heart of the sea, though its waters roar and foam*

*and the mountains quake with their surging...He
says, 'Be still and know that I am God...' "* (Ps.
46:1-3,10a).

Unfortunately, your world will change, your life fabric will unravel, and tragedies will come and shake you to your very core. You cannot stop the roaring storms, but that does not mean you have to be destroyed by them. You have an Anchor, a Rock, a Refuge, a Savior who is unshakable. The crumbling mountains, the roaring waters, the quaking earth—the most devastating of events have no effect on our Father. Be still and find him. Be still and know him. Be still and trust him. Be still.

Feeling like you'd rather run away than face the journey ahead of you? All you need is strength for today, for this moment:

*"Blessed are those whose strength is in you, whose
hearts are set on pilgrimage...They go from
strength to strength, till each appears before God
in Zion"* (Ps. 84:5,7).

When the road of grief stretches out indefinitely in front of you, set your heart on pilgrimage. Despite your broken heart, choose to embrace the journey as a chance to grow closer to the Lord. He cares for you infinitely more than you could ever imagine, and he will tend to your sorrow with gentle love. Don't panic at the impossible task ahead of you. Take this journey one day, one step, one breath at a time. Travel from strength to strength, accepting your daily bread from him and trusting that he will provide for you again tomorrow.

Welcome
to the Club

Welcome to the club.

I am so sorry you are here.

You've joined the ranks of those of us who have had to say an untimely goodbye. Loving and losing is nothing new to mankind, but there is a special kind of grief reserved for those who have lost much too young or far too soon. Now, there are many losses that fall under this category that I do not fully understand. I have not experienced the kind of devastation that comes with the loss of a spouse, parent, or child, and I can only imagine the heartbreak. But I do know that unexpected deaths leave you saying, "How could it be their time so soon? They had so much left to do here." Those kinds of losses leave behind a shocked, shattered collection of people who have no clue what to do next.

Our specific club chapter belongs to those of us who have lost a sibling at a young age.

I never wanted this, never dreamed I would be a member here. Yet here I am, somehow a part of the greeting committee. And I am determined not to let my membership here go to waste.

I promise to try my hardest never to say, "I know" or "I understand" to you. Because I don't *really* know. No one on earth can ever know the intimate details of the grief your heart now holds. That pain is unique to you, and the full knowledge of it rests solely between you and your Creator.

But I have walked the depths of this valley of despair. I know the feeling of frustration when you look around and realize nobody can ever truly know how your heart feels. And I know the feeling of relief when you look into the eyes of someone who understands even just a little because they are walking their own path of grief—relief at the fact that you don't have to struggle to put your pain into words for them; they just know.

Welcome to the club. Here we ask the whys and the hows, and we wrestle with anger, doubt, and fear. If your grief is making you feel crazy, you are in good company. At least we all get to be crazy together. Life looks different from our perspective in the club; we each have our own set of grief-colored glasses. Even in the midst of the blinding pain, we see the things that matter most in this world with a new, stunning clarity.

Welcome to the club where we never forget. When the noise of your crisis falls silent and the world turns the page onto a new chapter, we know your heart will be bookmarked on a certain page for the rest of your life. As time goes on, even those of us who should know better will have words fail us. We may say the wrong thing, or we might not say much at all, but our hearts beat fiercely with yours as the ones who have been left behind, the ones who will always remember.

As a fellow member, I promise to never tell you that everything happens for a reason. Because selfishly, I can't think of a reason in the world that would have made me want to go through these losses and join this club. I won't invalidate you by reasoning away your pain, but I do promise you that God can bring radiant beauty out of the ugliest, most horrifying brokenness. And we have a front row seat to witness that beauty.

Welcome to the club of those who feel sorrow more keenly than anyone else. Once grief has altered your life, your heart sinks every time you hear of a loss. Your stomach twists up, remembering the raw agony.

We spend our days feeling homesick for heaven, but you know what? We also hope harder than anyone else. We are the ones who spend the most time imagining the joy of heaven and counting down the tears until we reach the everlasting day of no more tears. The sweetest thing about being a member of this club is that we will have a very special greeting committee of our own dear ones waiting to welcome us when our race is complete.

So, welcome to the club. I wish with all my heart you weren't here, but I can promise you that you are not alone.

"Praise be to the God and Father of our Lord Jesus Christ, the Father of compassion and the God of all comfort, who comforts us in all our troubles, so that we can comfort those in any trouble with the comfort we ourselves receive from God"
(2 Cor. 1: 3-4).

CRAZY

IF YOU HAVE EVER EXPERIENCED GRIEF, YOU will be familiar with the predicament I am about to describe. I do not have a cute story or a thought-provoking analogy today, so I'm just going to jump right in with a confession. Here goes:

Grief makes me feel like I have flat-out lost my ever-loving mind.

There. I said it.

My mind, body, and emotions are so frequently stretched and pulled in so many different directions that I am not being dramatic when I say there are days when I literally (and I mean *literally*) feel like I am going to fall to pieces. Grief makes me crazy, and when I am feeling crazy, I simply cannot be logical, no matter how hard I try.

Let me give you some examples.

Example number one: My husband and I just bought our first house.

Logically, this should be a fun, exciting, and only surface-level stressful time. In reality, I am just a puddle of emotions about the whole thing. As I watched our rent house empty out and our new house filling up, I was constantly resisting the urge to frantically unpack all the boxes and put everything back the way it was. I think I probably cried more about leaving that house over a two-week stretch than I cried in a full two months of my grief. Why? Because we were living in that house when Lauren was still here. She saw that house, stayed in that house, and we had our last, beautiful, hours-long, sister talk in that house just a couple of months before the accident.

Logically, I know a house is just a house. But *emotionally*, I could not shake the feeling that our old house was a tie to Lauren—a tie that would be cut when we moved into a house she will never see or set foot in.

Logical? No. Crazy? Maybe. Honest feeling I can't help? Yes.

Example number two: I absolutely cannot make up my mind about how I feel.

Some days, nothing makes me more irrationally cranky than the words, "How are you?" My soul's deep down, honest-to-goodness gut reaction to that question is to silently cry out, "How do you think I am?" Isn't that a horrible thing to admit? I can be so tacky. But it gets worse. You know what else makes me irrationally cranky? When people fail to ask me how I am doing. I wish I was kidding.

Logically, I know when people check on me, it is because they love me. *Logically*, I know when people don't say anything, it is probably because they do not want to upset me or are afraid of saying the wrong thing.

In reality, there are just days where I cannot be pleased. I use the phrase "irrationally cranky" because I am fully aware of how fickle and irritable I am being, but that is just how I *feel* sometimes. Most days, I am so jumbled-up and stretched and pulled and tired and sad and stressed and distracted and whatever else, I could not even answer the question, "How are you?" if I were to ask myself.

Check on me? "Ugh." Don't check on me? "Ugh." Check on myself? "UGH."

Logical? Definitely not. Crazy? Definitely yes. Honest feeling I can't help? Absolutely.

Side note: PLEASE do not stop talking to me just because you read this and now know what a tacky person I can occasionally (okay, frequently) be. At the end of the day, I really and truly and desperately NEED people to talk to me and remember with me. I am really a nice person, I promise. Grief just makes me crazy sometimes.

Other crazy feelings:

Lonely, but sick of crowds.
Busy, but watching time stand still.
Afraid of moving on, but afraid of not moving on.
Smiling, laughing, participating in conversations, but numb inside.

Logical? Not at all. Crazy? Probably. Honest feelings I can't help? Most definitely.

The crazy thing about these crazy feelings is that I can spot them and define them for the illogical emotions that they are, but I cannot seem to stop having them. Some days I want up, some days I want down, and there does not seem to be a rhyme or reason to which days are which.

A crying baby cannot explain what it wants. It might want one thing one minute and something else the next. All a baby really knows when it cries is that it has some sort of discomfort, and it wants the hurt to stop. In the raw moments of my grief, I do not know what I need. All I want is for the hurt to stop.

This is not my first grief journey, so I know that all these illogical feelings are a normal part of the grief experience. We were created for life, and life to the *full*, so when we are faced with the jarring, harsh emptiness of death, our souls cry out at the wrongness of it. Part of the grief journey is learning how to reconcile the fullness of living when experiencing the emptiness of death, and I think we deserve extra helpings of grace when our grief makes us feel a little (or a lot) crazy.

So, yes. Grief makes me feel like I have lost my ever-loving mind. And I am slowly learning to ride these crazy waves out as they come. But if you happen to find my ever-loving mind for me, I will ever-love you. In the meantime, I will give myself some grace and rest in God's promises.

"Cast all your anxiety on him because he cares for you"
(1 Pet. 5:7).

HOW ARE YOU?

I FEEL LIKE I SPEND A LOT OF MY TIME TRYING to be tactful and sugarcoat things. I feel like I have to suppress parts of my grief because there are some things you just can't say out loud to other people. So, I sat down today and made a list of all the gut-level honest answers I currently have to the question, "How are you?"

Call it my 2016 State of the Union.

MY COMPLETELY HONEST LIST

* The question "how are you?" drives me crazy.

* The phrase "new normal" drives me crazy.

* There are a lot of days where I don't want to see anyone but my dog.

* I feel very isolated and lonely.

- Work is not a "nice distraction." There is not a single day where I would rather go to work than stay home.

- I'm not strong. I'm completely falling apart inside. I'm not sure I am even really functioning on the outside very well.

- I truly don't remember making it through the last few months. I just arrived here somehow.

- I would much rather end up crying because someone told me they miss my sister than keep it together and never know they held back because they were afraid of upsetting me.

- There are plenty of days I force myself to read the Bible or pray—not out of anger—my heart is just tired.

- Tragedy has struck my life so many times now that I secretly go around constantly expecting the other shoe to drop.

- I wonder what would have happened if I had died instead.

- I still imagine scenarios in my head about going back and changing one detail that would undo all of this. When I do that, I sometimes forget that you can't change the past.

- I don't feel any of the things I know to be true. I don't feel much of anything except exhaustion with occasional flashes of excruciating pain.

- Right now, I don't want to heal. I feel like healing is moving on, and moving on implies she was dispensable and replaceable—like I don't need her anymore.

- I stay in an almost constant state of being irritable and irrational. And I don't care.

- I worry about something happening to me and leaving my parents childless.

- I worry about when my parents pass away and I am the only family member left.

- Sometimes I feel guilty at the thought of growing old with my husband since Lauren didn't get to grow old with hers.

- Sometimes I feel guilty when I think about something else for a while. It's like I should have nothing but loss and grief on my mind all the time.

- The word "sister" breaks my heart now. I know the joy of having one, but I also know the excruciating pain of losing one and having to live without one.

- Sometimes I look at other families and wonder why they get to be together, whole, and happy when my family doesn't.

Here's the deal about writing out an honest list from time to time: if you always answer the question, "How are you?" with a simple "Fine," or even "Okay," you can start to internally lose touch with the real answers to that question. Some grieving people are comfortable honestly answering that question out loud to someone else. Other grieving people could not ever bring themselves in conversation to respond to that question with an honest answer. Let's be honest, most of the people who ask it would not know what to do with themselves if someone answered their question with complete honesty. Many of the honest answers aren't pretty; many of them may contradict themselves and make no sense. But it has been important to my own healing to unearth the answers to that question from time to time.

I have found that even if I can't answer a "How are you?" with complete honesty, sometimes it still helps me to go home and ask myself, "How am I?" and commit to being honest with myself in my answers. When I face the full reality of my grief, I can deal with the complex emotions as they come instead of stuffing them away and allowing them to fester and grow.

So, if you're up for a challenge, be brave with me today, and honestly answer the question, "How are you?"

Wordless Prayers

DESPERATELY BEGGING TO BE SPARED FROM looming heartbreak and loss.

Longing for the fulfillment of dreams and desires.

Trying to speak through a crushed heart and spirit.

Hannah had carried a heavy, weary, yearning heart for so long that her prayers had become wordless.

Her desperate prayers had gone unanswered for so many years that words had long since left her. All she had left was a steady stream of tears. All the thoughts she could muster were barely enough to move her lips in silence. All she had to offer was a broken heart that refused to relinquish the promises of God.

And still, she kept praying.

I read Hannah's story in 1 Samuel, and my heart marvels. How did she do it? How did she keep laying her heart and soul at the altar, begging for relief time after time, year after year? How did she keep coming back? How was she able to keep praying?

I've become afraid of fervently praying, afraid to open my heart and expose my deepest longings. If I don't put myself out there to ask, if I don't dare to hope, then I can't be let down.

Even so, my heart still cries out to God in wordless groans. Romans 8:26-27 tells us that *"...the Spirit helps us in our weakness. We do not know what we ought to pray for, but the Spirit himself intercedes for us through wordless groans. And he who searches our hearts knows the mind of the Spirit, because the Spirit intercedes for God's people..."*

He knows the deepest longings of my heart, just as he knew Hannah's. He does not expect me to know what to say. He is not waiting to hear how I pray before he decides how he wants to answer me. He just wants me to keep showing up. Even when my heart is so broken that I can't make any words come out.

It is okay if my prayers are wordless. When the Spirit intercedes for me in my wordless prayers, I can *"know that in all things God works for the good of those who love him, who have been called according to his purpose"* (Rom. 8:28).

IF NOT

"If we are thrown into the blazing furnace, the God we serve is able to deliver us from it, and he will deliver us from Your Majesty's hand. But even if he does not, we want you to know, Your Majesty, that we will not serve your gods or worship the image of gold you have set up" (Dan. 3:17-18).

AND IF NOT, HE IS STILL GOOD.

This thought has been unshakable for me lately. If not.

God's goodness is unfailing. It is not determined by the answer yes. It is not affected by whether or not I get the job I want or the happy life I wish for. Safe travels and good health are not indicators of how good God is. Sometimes tragedy strikes before you even get the chance to ask for what you want. How could such an event determine the goodness of our Creator? If it could, he would not be worthy.

God is good because he extends grace to the broken. He is good because he loves the unlovable. He is good because he offers hope to the hopelessly lost. God is good because of who he *is*.

God's goodness rests far above and out of reach of a simple yes or no. The broken circumstances of this world cannot touch the beautiful, bountiful goodness of God. I am so thankful for the fact that God is still good even when life is not. His goodness is the saving grace that carries me through each day.

"If not." Honestly, I don't like this concept. Sometimes it makes me angry; sometimes it makes me despair. "If not" is a hard statement of faith to make, and I'm still not very good at it. But I desperately want to be the kind of disciple who declares the goodness of God even in the darkest of circumstances. The answer is not always yes. But God is *always* good.

Lord, make me faithful.

New Year
(Courage)

At the beginning of 2016, I felt more afraid than I have ever felt in my life.

This fear surprised me. I honestly thought that the first Thanksgiving and the first Christmas without Lauren would be the hardest days I would face in my early grief. But those holidays were a blur of shock and disbelief. I was too numb to feel the extreme pain I was expecting. New Year's, however, caught me off guard.

Starting a new year usually signifies new beginnings, new possibilities, and untold promises. Not my new year. Instead of new beginnings, my year ahead was shadowed by an unexpected ending. New possibilities had lost their appeal for me because the year before had shown me that truly *anything* could happen. Rather than the optimism of untold promises, the new year held the despairing promise of pain, weariness, and loneliness. It was going to be a long year, and I was afraid.

I was afraid of facing the first year of my life I would ever live without my sister. I was afraid of time passing, day by day taking me further away from the last day I saw her, the last day I spoke with her. I was afraid of the good things that would come my way because I would not get to share them with Lauren. I was terrified of the hard things that were sure to come my way because my grief was already too heavy of a burden. How could I possibly carry even one more drop of pain when the tears I held in my heart were enough weight to crush me?

Have you ever felt that heavy, sightless, shapeless, overwhelming fear?

In the face of my fear and in desperate need of some foundational words of truth, I turned to the books and lessons of my childhood. In C.S. Lewis' novel, *The Voyage of the Dawn Treader*, there is a stunningly beautiful story that jumped off the pages and planted itself in my mind as I reread it.

On an adventure-seeking sea voyage, the characters find themselves sailing toward an unknown darkness on the horizon. Soon, that darkness is everywhere: before them, behind them, within them. In that darkness are their greatest fears and their worst nightmares. The terror is tangible, and the hopelessness is complete.

In desperation, when all seems lost, Lucy whispers a plea into the darkness for Aslan to help them. Soon after, an albatross (look up the symbolism of the albatross sometime...wow!) arrives and sings a wordless, pure, sweet song of hope. *"But no one except Lucy knew that as [the albatross] circled the mast it had whispered to her, 'Courage, dear heart,' and the voice, she felt sure, was Aslan's"* (Lewis 1952). The albatross then guides them out of the darkness back into warm, bright sunshine, clear blue skies, and the beautiful sea.

"Courage, dear heart."

Just soak in that for a minute.

Courage, dear heart, you are not alone.

Courage, dear heart, this darkness will not overcome you.

Courage, dear heart, even an entire sea of despair cannot drown out the sweet, song of hope from the King.

Courage, dear heart, the greatest fear you face is mist and shadows compared to the solid, bright truth you have been promised.

Courage, dear heart, there are brilliant, beautiful, joyful days ahead.

"Courage, dear heart."

I cannot tell you how tightly I have clung to these words, to this thought, over the past year. Yet, these words that I hold as an anchor within me do not mean that I no longer battle fear.

I still wrestle with anxiety every single time someone I love travels. Doubts, worries, and whispers of terrible possibilities begin to creep into the edges of my mind and weave themselves into my imagination.

The siren of an ambulance still makes my entire body tense up. In those moments, I am unable to suppress the image of the emergency vehicles that raced to the scene on a dark, Texas highway in the middle of the night, coming upon a battered car with one passenger clinging to life and one already gone.

I am terrified at the thought of losing more of the people I hold dear. I am afraid of remembering too much about the painful events, and I fear forgetting too many special memories.

When I think about the years I have ahead of carrying this heavy grief and fear, I am overwhelmed. And in those moments of immense fear, my heart cries out for help. Without fail, I hear the echoes of a promise for deliverance: *"Courage, dear heart."*

Whispered prayers for deliverance are always answered, but that does not always mean immediate relief. Being led out of this kind of darkness is a journey.

Sometimes those answers come in the form of a single extra ounce of strength to keep holding on for one more minute. Sometimes those answers look like a strong arm or shoulder to lean on as you take another trembling step forward. And sometimes that answer is the small, quiet whisper of, "*Courage, dear heart,*" in your weakest, darkest, most hopeless moments. And little by little, step by step, moment by moment, you sail ever closer to the promise of light and warmth and joy.

So, today I just want to tell you this:

I know the darkness hurts; I know it makes you feel afraid. I know it seems hopeless sometimes, but don't give up. Light is coming. Hold on for those clear, blue skies.

"I have told you all this so that you may have peace in me. Here on earth you will have many trials and sorrows. But take heart, because I have overcome the world" (John 16:33 NLT).

Counseling

About a month ago, I caved in and finally took the terrifying, vulnerable step of going to a counselor. I was stretched too thin, down to my very fibers, and those fibers were fraying and unraveling. It wasn't just that my grief was too much; it was all too much for me. Turning off the alarm and willing myself to get out of bed every morning. Sitting at my desk job for eight hours a day. Thinking about what I had at home that could provide sustenance for an evening. Forget about having a meal, we just needed fuel to make it through the next exhausting day. Career stress, life decisions, broken air conditioners, cars that needed repairs. I was not living; I was existing, and I was barely even managing that. It was all just too much for me.

My last attempt at going to counseling was a disaster. The hurt from that experience and my dread of having to start over with someone new and endure the reliving and retelling of my story made me wait over a year before going again. But I've been feeling pretty desperate these days, so I took the plunge.

We talked about my story. We talked about my stretching thin, my broken remains of a life and the particular, crucial pieces that I'm now missing. And finally, I put into words a feeling from one of the deepest, most bruised, broken, wounded places in my aching soul:

"I still believe in the goodness and faithfulness of God. I believe he is sovereign, and I trust him. But I don't believe in miracles anymore. Not for me. They happen for other people, but not in my life. I'm afraid to pray for things anymore because the answer seems to always be no. And my heart just can't take any more hits like that."

I whispered those hopeless words with silent tears of defeat slipping down my face. I don't want to think those things or feel that way, but I do. Yet somehow, putting those secret thoughts of despair into words and saying them out loud seemed to lessen their power over me by just the tiniest fraction. Admitting my hopelessness and unbelief aloud ignited a small spark, a tiny flicker of hope that maybe God was waiting for me to say it so that he could prove me wrong.

I'm still stretched too thin. I'm still overwhelmed. I'm still so messed up and broken. But I said some things that I needed to say.

And now I've got that tiny flicker of hope. So, that's a start.

Missing You

Dear Lauren,

I miss you. How many times did you used to say that to me? And I missed you too, but I also stayed so busy that I didn't think about it as much. But I get it now. I think I'm busier than ever, but in the chaos, all I can think about is you.

I want to talk to you about the people who drive me crazy. I want to send you pictures of my latest home improvement projects. I miss how you just got me, and how you thought I could do anything even when I wasn't sure that I could. I miss feeling like the world's greatest comedian around you because you thought all my dumb jokes and weird voices were hilarious. I miss comparing newlywed notes with you because boys are weird and hard to live with sometimes. I want to compare future baby names with you. I miss our family group text full of nothing but dog pictures.

I just miss you. I miss giving you shopping advice. I miss buying you birthday and Christmas presents. I miss you at big family gatherings and at small family dinners. I miss having you to share our growing up stories with and I miss the memories we never got to make.

I still talk about you all the time because you are still a foundational part of my life, but I miss having new stories and life updates to share about you.

One of our friends announced last night that she is pregnant. I was so happy for her, but then I was just flooded with a slow sadness. I wished it was you. I wished our lives were moving along the way we planned them: progressing through these joyful milestones the way everyone else's lives seem to do. And then that deep ache of missing you rose to the surface. That ache will be my close companion today. I can tell it isn't ready to ease, but I'll take it. It means I still carry you with me. It means I had something so lovely and precious that it is worth the slow sadness and the deep ache now that I don't have it anymore.

I feel like it was just yesterday that I was talking to you and making holiday plans with you, but I think that was just another me in another lifetime. So much has happened that I need to tell you about. But as much as I have to tell you, I know there is an eternity's worth more to hear about what YOU have been up to!

So, let's get together soon, okay? I need some sister time.

All my love,
Lindsey

Choosing Joy

I STRUGGLE WITH THE THOUGHT OF CHOOSING joy. For months, I have nursed the wounds of my heart (rightfully so, I think) and fully embraced the depths of my sorrow. I have been handed a burden that I did nothing to deserve.

But whispers of caution have begun to stir up in my heart—whispers that remind me not to live my whole life as a victim. What has happened to my family will always be a tragedy; nothing will ever make it okay. But if I let it permanently turn me into a victim then I give Satan a victory. Tragedies happen all the time to people all around the world. Though forever marked by my loss and grief, I am not defined by this tragedy. I am defined by how I choose to respond.

To choose joy feels wrong. Almost like if I am able to have joy, Lauren must not have meant that much to me. If I am able to feel happy, this tragedy must not have shattered my life after all. But Lauren meant everything to me; she was <u>part</u> of me, my only sister. November 24, 2015 is the nightmare from which I will never awake.

Every moment of my life from this time onward will lack a bit of the richness and fullness it should have had. Without the specific seasoning Lauren brought to my life, each dish I taste will be a little bland.

But there is a growing longing inside of me. I am so very tired and weary of being tired and weary. I don't want to be sad every single day anymore. I am tired of this steady diet of heavy, bitter grief. I want to taste joy again, even if its sweetness is tainted with some bitterness.

Choosing joy doesn't mean I won't wake up and feel sad some days. It doesn't even mean that I have officially put away my grief and never let it weigh me down again. Choosing joy doesn't mean I've forgotten Lauren. On the contrary, choosing joy helps me to remember Lauren better and more fully. Choosing joy means I don't let Satan turn me into a victim. It means God gets the glory and victory out of this tragedy.

Lord, give me the courage to choose joy.

AROUND THE TABLE

WHAT A YEAR. WHAT A GRUELING, GROWING, heartbreaking, hope-clinging, exhausting, learning, wrestling, humbling, walking-by-faith-not-by-sight year.

To be completely honest, it feels a bit cruel that the one-year anniversary of Lauren's passing falls on Thanksgiving Day. As I have thought about the approach of this day, my heart has cried out, "How?" How, on a day specifically set aside for gratitude and gathering with loved ones, am I supposed to be able to muster a heart of thanks? But truthfully, I've been asking the question, "How?" for a whole year now. How is this possible? How are we expected to bear this? How can another month have already passed? How am I going to survive this week? How am I going to endure this day? How am I going to make it through the next few moments of searing pain? *How?*

Sometimes thankfulness is something that naturally overflows, and sometimes it is something you just have to practice. In my mother's family we have a special tradition we call "Grandad Prayers." When we gather for a meal, my Grandad has us go around the table and take turns saying what we are thankful for and then praying as a family. Today, I'm going to take you around my table and tell you who I see that makes me thankful even on a day of sorrow like today.

At my table, I see my husband, Heath. What a gift of light he has been to me in this dark year. Heath is my strong and steady—the rock solid to my wild and crazy wind—and he has continually served me and loved me to carry me through this year. I daily witness the hands and feet of Christ through Heath.

Next at the table, I see my parents. Their faithfulness and graciousness this year have astounded me. I have always been proud to be their daughter, but watching them react to this tragedy in committed faith has humbled me and made me feel incredibly honored to be their daughter. We continue to cling to each other on this journey.

I see Trent. In a word, I would describe Trent as brave. The man who fell in love with my beautiful sister and made her his wife woke up in a hospital one day to find he had lost his future with her. I cannot fathom the amount of courage and trust it takes Trent to hold tightly to his faith in God. Yet, Trent does so much more than that; he boldly proclaims his faith, and he takes the time to stop and encourage countless others along the way. What an honor to know a man like Trent.

Under my table (because I really would be a crazy dog mom if I let him sit at the table) I have to mention my dog, Darcy, who pulls all seventy pounds of himself into my lap to kiss me and cuddle me when I can't stop crying. He always manages to bring a smile back to my face. Lauren was a firm believer in the medicinal power of dog cuddles, and sometimes I think she is sending me hugs and kisses through Darcy.

Around my table, I see my grandparents, the most faithful prayer warriors I know, covering my family in prayer each and every day. I see the dear friends who sat and wept with me when there were no words to be said. I see the childhood friend who left gifts on my porch every month this past year. I see the people who sent me handwritten notes, let me vent, or continued to check in with me as the chaos quieted down and the silent, grief-filled months slowly passed by.

Lastly, the seat at my table closest to my heart today is Lauren's. Although today will forever mark the date of loss and anguish for my family, in a strange way, November 24th will always serve as a day of deep gratitude for me. I rejoice that being Lauren's sister is a role that nobody in the whole world could ever fill but me. Her existence is woven into my own identity, and her life was so much a part of mine that even her loss continues to shape me.

Today, I am desperately thankful that this world is not my home. Today, I am humbled and filled with gratitude that I serve a God who comforts, heals, and gives hope to the brokenhearted. I am so thankful to have tasted the beautiful sweetness of the Lord even amidst my steady diet of bitter grief this year. I cannot fathom enduring this swirling mess of confusion and despair without the promise of a better, brighter, joy-filled future. My life here and now is the mist and shadows; the life Lauren is experiencing right now is more real, more tangible, and more true than I could ever imagine. So yes, Lauren will always have a seat around my mist-and-shadows table, but the knowledge that gives me gratitude even on a day like today is the fact that she is saving me a seat around a much better table.

I imagine each meal the disciples shared together after the death and resurrection of Jesus was a little bittersweet. Don't you know as they broke bread together, their hearts must have ached with the memories and missing their dear friend and mentor? But they didn't stop meeting around the table simply because he was no longer physically with them. In fact, his absence made gathering around the table even more vital.

Not every meal around the table is joyful, but every meal around the table is important. It is around the table that we take our place in a tradition as old as mankind. There at the table—in the middle of the passing plates and talking over the top of each other, in between the breaking bread and the sharing stories—we catch a glimpse of that which is simple, pure, and good.

So, with one year behind us and a lifetime ahead of us, what do we do now? How do we do this? We continue to gather around the table. Around the table, the noise of the world fades and our focus is shifted from the mist and shadows back to the real and bright.

"I thank my God every time I remember you"
(Philippians 1:3).

Saying Goodbye

Sometimes I wonder what it would have been like if I had gotten to say goodbye. If I had known it was coming.

It might have given me a little more closure. I might have fewer dreams that it never happened. But plenty of people get lots of time, too much time, to say goodbye, and I'm not sure that would be any easier. They witness their loved one suffering; they see the decline, the struggle. And those images will stay with them as they grieve, long after the goodbye is over.

I don't think there is ever a painless way to say goodbye.

Scripture tells us that God set eternity in the heart of man. (Ecclesiastes 3:11 paraphrase) Saying goodbye goes against our very nature. We are designed for eternity, and that makes endings feel inherently wrong and backward to us.

In 2 Kings, Elisha knows Elijah is going to be with God, and he clings to his side until the very last moment.

Prophets warned him they would soon be separated, and Elisha tells them, *"Yes, I know…so be quiet"* (2 Kgs. 2:3). Elijah keeps telling Elisha to stay behind while he goes on his final journey, and Elisha's response is always the same: *"As surely as the LORD lives and as you live, I will not leave you"* (2 Kgs. 2:2,4,6).

As long as you have life and breath, I will not leave your side. Until the Lord himself takes you from this earth, I will not be separated from you.

And when Elijah asks Elisha what he can do for him before he leaves, Elisha doesn't have to think twice about his request. *"Let me inherit a double portion of your spirit"* (2 Kgs. 2:9).

I'm not strong enough to go on without you. I don't have what it takes. I need twice as much spirit as you had just to be able to fill your shoes and move forward.

Elijah is whisked away into heaven in a chariot of fire, and Elisha is left behind, watching and grieving. When he could no longer see anything, Elisha stoops down and picks up Elijah's cloak. Think of the stories that came with that cloak: the cloak that Elijah pulled over his face when he heard the still, small whisper of God outside the cave in Mt. Horeb (1 Kgs. 19:13), the cloak that Elijah threw over Elisha as he called him into the Lord's service (1 Kgs. 19:19), and the cloak Elijah used to perform miracles (2 Kgs. 2:8). Elisha picks up the cloak and carries it with him. Elijah will forever be a part of him; Elijah's stories and legacy will live on in Elisha.

When I wonder what things would have been like if I had known the goodbye was coming, I know I would have clung to them like Elisha clung to Elijah.

I texted Anabel that Friday morning and I also left her a very lengthy voicemail (as was our custom) as I walked back to my dorm from class. I talked with Lauren on the phone that Tuesday night, just hours before her accident. I didn't know those would be my last communications with either one of them. There would have been so much more to say if I had known. But I did tell them both that I loved them. I am forever thankful for that.

As much as I grieve being separated from them, I know I carry their stories with me. As I pick up the pieces and move forward, they come along wrapped around my shoulders, giving me warmth, comfort, and strength for the days ahead.

WHISPERS OF A GRIEVING HEART

Forget me not, for I still weep,
My heart still mourns and vigil keeps.

Forget me not, though I seem strong,
My silent ache makes days grow long.

Forget me not, my courage fails
When waves of grief and doubt assail.

Forget me not when moments come,
For all my moments miss someone.

Forget me not from day to day,
My days have changed, my loss remains.

Forget me not as time moves on,
For time cannot replace what's gone.

Forget me not when joy returns,
For joy tastes bittersweet, I've learned.

"Forget them not!" my heart now cries,
"Don't let their loss erase their life."

Forget me not,
Forget them not,
For I cannot forget.

If Only

Lately, I've had a pretty bad case of the "if onlys."

Sometimes they sprinkle down, pitter-pattering across my mind. "If only...if only..."

If only I could share this sweet moment with her. If only I could send her a text or pick up the phone and call her.

Sometimes their sharpness stabs and twists.

If only I had acted differently. If only I could talk to her one more time. If only I could share these new milestones with her and confide secrets, both joyful and sorrowful, to her. If only I could seek wisdom from her steady, gentle spirit.

Sometimes they pile up into a mountain of how things could have been different.

If only she had left a minute sooner or later. If only we had known in time to prevent it.

Sometimes they howl and writhe in pain.

If only it had been me. If only I could have taken her place. If only I could erase the images in my mind.

Sometimes their whispers echo through the heart.

If only she was here, everything would be perfect.

Martha and Mary wrestled with the "if onlys," too. *"Lord, if only you had been here, my brother would not have died"* (John 11:21, 32 NLT).

Jesus' response to them is profound: *"I am the resurrection and the life. Anyone who believes in me will live, even after dying. Everyone who lives in me and believes in me will never ever die"* (John 11:25-26 NLT).

The other day I was aching so badly to talk to her that I sat down and wrote her a letter. I poured out my heart the way only a sister can to a sister, and at the end I asked her this: *"Tell me the end is worth it, Lauren. Because right now it doesn't feel like it."*

As I thought about her and all that we shared during her years here, I felt certain this would be her reply: "If only you could see. If only you could experience the fullness of the glory of God. If only you could share in the music of the heavenly chorus. If only you could taste the sweetness of his presence. If only you were here. You would know 'worth it' doesn't even begin to cover it."

So, when the "if onlys" start to crowd in, I'll remember that they have no power over the Resurrection and the Life.

THE DIVINE GIFT
OF COMFORT

LAUREN'S ACCIDENT HAPPENED ON THE Tuesday before Thanksgiving. We woke up to the news early Wednesday morning, and we turned around and drove home instead of completing our holiday travels as planned. On Thanksgiving Day, while everyone we knew was celebrating with their families, safe, happy, and whole, my parents and I sat down to plan my sister's funeral.

After lunchtime that day, they started to come. I don't remember who came first. Honestly, I don't remember most of the faces of those who came at all. I just remember thinking what a strange juxtaposition it was as the people began to fill my parents' house—freshly full of food, family, and warmth—visiting the freshly emptied, cold, and broken.

They came because they loved my family. They came and they sat, and they offered words and tears and hugs. But I just wanted to slip away and hide where they couldn't find me. My world was shattered beyond repair. I didn't want the condolences that poured out of their full bellies and their full hearts on a day specifically set aside for being thankful. I just couldn't find it in my heart to be thankful at all.

The book of Job is one that so many people turn to when they face crisis or tragedy in their lives. He did nothing to deserve his losses; in fact, he received his trials because of his outstanding faithfulness. But I want to talk about Job's friends. The Bible says they gathered to comfort him and wept aloud at the sight of him in his grief. *"Then they sat on the ground with him for seven days and seven nights. No one said a word to him, because they saw how great his suffering was"* (Job 2:13). They got off to such a great start.

But as time passes, they can no longer sit quietly, and they begin to fill Job's broken-hearted silence with words and opinions. They attempt to make sense of his circumstances. They preach to Job about the way they believe God works and how Job should be reacting to his misfortunes. They point fingers and talk of things of which they have no understanding.

After a great deal of back and forth, Job finally says to them, *"You are miserable comforters, all of you! Will your long-winded speeches never end? What ails you that you keep on arguing? I also could speak like you, if you were in*

*my place; I could make fine speeches against you and shake
my head at you. But my mouth would encourage you; comfort from my lips would bring you relief"* (Job 16:2-5).

What is it that makes us blurt out the worst words at
the worst times? I have been guilty of it countless times
myself. We feel desperate to say something, *anything*,
that will alleviate the pain. I thought after walking my
own grief journeys that I would be better at sitting in
silence with someone else who is hurting. Yet, even
though I know better, I find myself turning into what
Job called a "miserable comforter" and trying to come
up with something profound to say that will make
it better.

But there are a holy, sacred few people who just sit in
silence with you as long as you need. They don't try
to fix it, they just weep with you. They choose their
words humbly and carefully, never implying that they
understand your pain, but simply that they ache with
you. Those are the people who never get up and walk
away. Those are the ones who, years later, will still
listen to you hash out the same twisted mess of your
grief again and again and never stop you or tell you
that you've said those things to them before. Those
are the ones who not only remember anniversaries but
also check in with you the other 364 days of the year
because they know you can never escape or forget your
loss like the rest of the world can.

I truly believe those types of people have a divine gift of comfort. Those are the people whose words I hunger to hear in the midst of the outpouring of words from the general public.

They are the ones like my father-in-law who said to me, "I don't understand, and I don't think I ever will. I just keep praying, 'Lord, make me faithful.'" When he said that, he was telling me I didn't have to reconcile what happened and be okay with it; I just needed God's grace to keep me faithful in my grief.

Or like my mother-in-law, who admitted to me that she doesn't always know what to say, but she wanted me to know that she never forgets my loss. She put me at ease to bring up Lauren whenever I feel like it.

Or like one of my college professors who prayed, "Lord, come quickly," and still checks in with me from time to time, years later, when most have moved on with life.

It was the simple, sweet, heartfelt words that stuck with me long after my moment of crisis had passed and as I transitioned into the long, lonely season of grief that followed.

We have all said the wrong thing at the wrong time. Even with my years of experience wrestling with grief, I still find myself stumbling for words when someone

I know takes their first steps on the pathway of loss. I somehow feel extra pressure to say something helpful because I know more than most what they are feeling in those raw, anguishing, early moments of grief. I think I will spend the rest of my life reminding myself of what I found to be the most comforting in my time of deep grief.

When in doubt, silent or simple support is a great place to start.

Note:

Ironically, my first draft of this essay was titled, "If You Can't Say Anything Nice," and it was not the nicest essay I have ever written. I included some of the *unhelpful* things that were said to me by some classic "miserable comforters." After reading the finished draft, I decided this book was not the place to dwell on those words. My heart felt a lot more peace as I rewrote the essay, focusing instead on some things people said that *did* help me.

Also, I need to clarify that this concept is based on my personal grief perspective. Not everyone wants the same thing. Some people need LOTS of talking to process. But I would still recommend that you take your cues from them and give them the freedom of choosing to whom they want to open their hearts. Don't flood them with words until you are sure they want to hear them in that moment. In general, I think that most grieving people would agree that less is more.

Yes and No

"Coming up behind Jesus, she touched the fringe
of his robe. Immediately, the bleeding stopped"
(Luke 8:44 NLT).

THE GIRL WAS SICK. AFTER TWELVE SHORT
years of life, she was running out of time. And her
parents knew it. No amount of money or power or
status could fix this.

The woman was sick. After twelve long years of noes,
she was out of money, out of options, and on her very
last strand of hope.

Out of desperation, the girl's father gave it his last shot
and fell at the feet of the healing rabbi. "Please. I know
I don't deserve your help. I'm not worthy. But I beg
you—come save my daughter."

Out of desperation, the woman pushed her way through
a crowd of people. "I'm not worthy of his attention.
No one wants to sit through this pain with me anymore. But if I could just reach out to the tip of my

grasp, if I could just brush my fingers across the hem of his clothes—maybe, just maybe I could get a taste of relief."

On his way to heal a twelve-year-old girl, Jesus stops to heal a twelve-year-old illness. And in the time he takes to look into the desperate woman's eyes and give her the joyful yes for which she had spent years begging, the parents of the girl received a devastating no.

"Don't worry about coming anymore. She's gone. There isn't anything anyone can do. You were our last hope for a yes, but no one gets victory over death."

Yes and *no*.

Those answers have tormented me. The question doesn't just stop at, "Why do bad things happen to good people?" It becomes, "Why was my answer *no* when their answer was *yes*? I've been praying just as desperately. I love you just as much. How can you make the decision of who to stop and heal and who to let slip away?"

Two people in a car accident. One lives and the other does not.

Two people diagnosed with a disease. One beats it back, and the other beats us all home.

Two struggling marriages. One overcomes and emerges stronger, while the other falls apart.

Two lives. One filled with joy and purpose, and the other struggling to make it through a single day.

Yesses and *noes* are everywhere, but sometimes it seems like *noes* are much more common.

When you're heartbroken from a *no*, you look around you and feel like everyone else is getting the *yes* they asked for. And then all of a sudden, your *no* starts to feel very personal. What is the rhyme or reason for who gets a miracle and who goes into mourning? How do you remain faithful through a *no* while watching others receive a *yes*?

Because it feels like that, doesn't it? That for God to take the time to stop and answer someone's prayers, he must turn his back on someone else's. That the people who receive *noes* just slip through the cracks because he can't save everyone at once.

But just because it feels that way does not mean it is true.

Yesses and *noes* are not a competition. It is not the fastest or the smartest or the best people who get to God first and claim all the *yesses*. God does not have a limited amount of goodness to disperse before he runs out. *"His compassions are new every morning..."* (Lam. 3:22-23 paraphrase).

Noes can be devastating. I don't ever want to disregard the pain of living in a *no*. Some *noes* stay with you for the rest of your life, and no amount of *yesses* later down the road will make the heartbreak of that one *no* go away. I live with the *no* of missing my sister every single day.

Sometimes, you find yourself in the middle of a season where the *noes* just seem to keep coming. *Noes* often love company. They tend to arrive in groups, one after another, until your heart cries out that one more *no* will shatter it beyond repair. And as you look around at all the *yesses* everyone else seems to be getting, it makes you despair of ever getting a *yes* again. You start to think that perhaps *no* is just your lot in life.

But hear me: you are not condemned to a lifetime of *noes*.

After a series of heartbreaking *noes* in my life, I had to work hard to relearn the lesson that God loves to give good gifts to his children. (Matt. 7:11) I was afraid to pray because I assumed the answer would be *no*. My heart couldn't take any more grief and disappointment, so I just quit asking.

But just because I didn't receive the *yes* I once desperately prayed for does not mean I am forgotten or that my pain goes unnoticed. There is far more to our story than we could ever know or comprehend.

Yeses and *noes* do not affect the goodness of God. Although your world may be crumbling around you, the God of the Universe is steadfastly on his throne. *"When the foundations are being destroyed, what can the righteous do? The LORD is in his holy temple; the LORD is on his heavenly throne"* (Ps. 11:3-4).

God is always working. When all hope is lost for the little girl's family, Jesus takes the girl by the hand and calls her back to life. In that moment, scripture says *"her spirit returned"* to her (Luke 8:55). There is not a *no* in this broken world that can push you beyond the reach of God's comfort and healing.

You may feel like your *no* has removed all traces of life from your body—that you are just an empty shell. But the touch of God has the power to return your spirit. This *no* will not claim victory over your life. You will smile and laugh and breathe deeply and fully again. Even the most final of *noes* in this life will become a *yes* in eternity.

So, maybe life isn't meant to be viewed as a series of *yesses* and *noes*. Because that turns God's sole purpose into being a wish-fulfiller, and that makes him far too small. Maybe life is meant to be a daily pursuit of his presence, his touch. Only his touch can soothe the ache as we wait what feels like a lifetime for relief. If you seek him as you wait, you will find yourself straining and reaching in times of feast and in times of famine just to touch the hem of his garment, just to live even in the threshold of his kingdom. (Ps. 84:10 paraphrase)

He is there in the waiting, there in the longing, there in the reaching, there in the healing, there in the disappointment, there in the hopelessness, there in the rejoicing.

THESE THREE REMAIN

"And now these three remain: faith, hope and love.
But the greatest of these is love" (1 Cor. 13:13).

THESE THREE REMAIN.

Not much remains when you have lost someone. Joy is gone. Plans and dreams are gone. Future memories yet to be made are gone. Passion is gone. Strength, energy, drive, and courage all disappear. Words fail. Any and all things with even a trace of goodness seem to be gone. But these three remain.

Faith.

Faith is believing that the sun will rise once more even when the night is oppressively dark and long. Faith is believing in the unfailing goodness of God when life is unbearably bad. Faith *"is confidence in what we hope for and assurance about what we do not see"* (Heb. 11:1). When blinded by despair, I cling to my faith that there are things I cannot see. This is not a foolish, wishful, made-up thought to deny reality. This is a deep conviction, an assurance, that there is more to life than enduring this broken world. If there weren't more, why would our hearts cry out against the wrongness of the losses we encounter?

When nothing is left, when I cannot see, I choose to hold fast to my faith.

Hope.

Hope is the only substance that can fill the emptiness. Hope is the only weapon that can battle the bitter, overwhelming despair. Hope is the whisper of a promise of restoration and redemption. Hope does not erase the current pain, but it holds the key to healing. Hope is the only thing that enables you to get out of bed each day and put one foot in front of the other. Hope is the belief of better days ahead, of a bright, beautiful eternity free of grief.

When life washes over me and threatens to drift me into the deep, hopeless waters of despair, I cling to hope, the *"anchor for [my] soul,"* and I *"hold unswervingly...for he who promised is faithful"* (Heb. 6:19, 10:23).

Love.

"But the greatest of these is love." Love carries us when we are too weak to carry on. Love reaches through the darkness and promises light. Love refuses to give up. Love transforms brokenness into beauty. Love comes to us as the hands and feet of God's people, ministering to our needs and weeping and mourning with those of us who weep and mourn. When all other things fail, love is everlasting. Even faith and hope find their foundation in love.

Someday, when we come face to face with the Ultimate Love, the need for faith and hope will be removed. Those we have loved and lost far too early are now in glory, seeing the full realization of their faith and hope. There is no need for trust in the unseen when all is clearly, beautifully evident. There is nothing left to hope for when all the goodness our hearts have ever desired surrounds us. But love: love is unmistakable, unfailing, and unending. Just stop and think about it: the all-surpassing, glorious, worthy, faithful, pure, brilliant, sacrificial, everlasting, holy, joyous, radiant, eternal love. The love we encounter here on earth is but a glimpse of the great love that is to come.

When there is nothing left, these three remain.

This faith does not come because I am strong. I cling to it because I have no strength.

This hope does not come because I am wise. I hold to it fiercely because I don't know any other way to survive.

This love, oh, this love, is beyond what I could ever deserve. This love is the only thing I know to be true.

Lord, come quickly.

LEFT BEHIND

I PRETTY MUCH CAME OUT OF THE WOMB trying to keep up with my sister. Anything she was old enough to do, so was I: reading, going to school, riding a bike without training wheels...you name it. I had to run faster to keep up with my sister and cousins in our summertime games of kick-the-can. I had to get up earlier than everyone else if I wanted my chance at the best cereal when we had breakfast with my grandparents. I had to read big books and learn bigger words so I could play Taboo with the rest of my family. Maybe there is a little bit of that spirit in all younger siblings, but I will freely admit that I have an extra dose of determination to never EVER get left behind.

Lauren was the best kind of big sister. She let me tag along with her and her friends. She learned cursive in school and promptly came home and taught me. She walked me through each stage of life and championed my cause. Pretty much anything she did, she told me I could do too. The older we got, the more our paths aligned, and Lauren, always one step ahead of me, showed me the way through college, graduation, first jobs, engagement, wedding planning, and the newlywed life. Dreams of future babies, family holidays and trips, and even the "dreaded" gray hair and wrinkles filled my vision for the future, filling my heart with gratitude. I knew Lauren would always be there, learning, sharing, and walking beside me through each milestone.

Then, one night, I went to bed with one future ahead of me and I woke up the next morning to the harsh reality of a very different future. Lauren was gone. Over the following days, weeks, and months as I grieved and processed, one of the questions that kept resounding through my heart was, "What do I do now?" I have always had Lauren's footsteps to follow. How on earth am I supposed to keep living? I am the baby of the family; I have never known a life where I did not have my big sister.

There are many facets of grief that are hard to put a name to, hard to define. I wrestled with this aspect of my grief. I tangled and untangled, moaned and groaned, and wept in anguish and frustration. I could not wrap my head around it. Then, in September of the next year, my family experienced another loss. My uncle, David Rickard, passed away. Once more, I sat in the family section of a funeral for someone who left far too early. Once more, I stood in a cemetery and felt the waves of loneliness surging deep within my soul. I felt that particular hopeless, nameless pain that accompanies the "What nows?" and the "How am I supposed to go ons?" in moments like those. On the road as we drove home from David's services, the stark truth behind my wrestling finally hit me:

I am so very weary of being left behind.

Deep down in my bones, weary. All my life, I have fought to keep up. One by one, I see the most wonderful people I know leave this world behind, and I cannot do a thing to keep up with them. This is one thing I can't work harder at or practice more to catch up; I've been left behind.

I think about when Jesus ascended into heaven. His disciples just stood staring after him into the sky. And you know something? I think I get it. These men spent years of their lives with Jesus. They shared meals together, they traveled together, they walked and talked and laughed and cried and learned and grew together. Because of Jesus, these men saw the world through transformed eyes. One day, they were sharing a Passover meal at the feet of their mentor, the bright and hopeful future lying before them. Then, in one horrible night, that dream of the future was destroyed.

Devastation, anguish, disbelief. Have you been there?

Then, in one glorious, incomprehensible, miracle morning, that future was restored to them. They spent the next few weeks soaking in every encounter with their dear friend. He showed them a new future—brighter and more beautiful than they could have imagined. Yet, all too soon, the time came for him to leave. And his most beloved friends were left behind, staring into the sky with deepest longing.

In their minds, they knew the truth of his Kingdom. They believed in his promise that they would reunite in eternal joy. But, obviously, their hearts were struggling to catch up with their minds because all they could do was stare at the empty space where they last saw him. If you have grieved, you are familiar with this feeling. It is a cliff-hanger, unfinished, lurching, lost, incomplete, homesick, yearning sort of feeling.

After a gentle nudge from the angels, the disciples went on to spread the gospel to the world with passion burning in their hearts. But I have a hunch that from time to time, they all found themselves staring into the sky, wishing with all their hearts that they didn't have to stay behind anymore.

Scripture says, *"Where, O death, is your sting?"* (1 Cor. 15:55). Every time I read those words or hear them sung in church, my heart cries out, "It's right over here! I feel it!" The sting of death cannot touch those who have gone on, so it lies with those of us who are left behind in this broken world. We know the truth of the future; it cannot be taken from us.

Death may not have victory over my life, but boy, it sure does sting sometimes.

I think that's okay to admit, don't you? We have work to do, truth to share, and love to spread. But on the days when the passion and energy are running a little low, it is that yearning, left-behind feeling that gives us a reminder and a reason to keep going.

So, on the days when you find yourself with a longing and homesick heart, staring up into the sky, out the window, or at an empty chair, give yourself some grace. If the disciples can do it, so can you. It stings a little to get left behind, but the sweet future in store for us will wipe those tears and turn those lonely, longing sighs into joyful, jubilant singing.

"He will wipe every tear from their eyes. There will be no more death or mourning or crying or pain, for the old order of things has passed away"
(Rev. 21:4).

JONATHAN AND DAVID

WHEN I THINK ABOUT MY FRIENDSHIP WITH Anabel, I think about Jonathan and David. Scripture tells us that Jonathan loved David *"as his own soul"* (1 Sam. 18:1 ESV). Sometimes in life, you come across a once-in-a-lifetime friendship, and even from the very beginning, you know you have been given something incredibly rare and special.

I felt that way about Anabel. Now, she was a remarkable person on her own, but I had never experienced a friendship like ours before. And I have never found one like it since. (I feel the need to stop here and make a note that I have been blessed with several friendships that I would classify as "once-in-a-lifetime" relationships, and each one of them is beautifully unique and infinitely dear to my heart.) Anabel and I were very different in many ways, but we were kindred spirits. When we became friends, my heart simply clicked with hers. I felt challenged by her and I looked up to her, yet I also felt like we were equals. We talked about anything and everything from the silliest stories to the deep, heart-wrenching moments of our lives.

When my world was turning upside down and I felt overwhelmed by my fears, I slipped outside into my backyard to call Anabel. She spoke truth, love, and encouragement to me, and I felt like I was not alone. When I was about to burst with the most exciting news, Anabel was the first person I wanted to call. She rejoiced with me so well, it was as if the good news was her own. I felt safe and loved in my friendship with Anabel. I was free to be fully myself, yet by Anabel just being herself, she made me want to strive to be better each day.

When Jonathan and David part ways for the last time in 1 Samuel 20, they pour out their hearts to each other. They recognize that God has been the foundation of their friendship, and Jonathan asks David to remember his household even as David steps into his new life as the new king of Israel. As they said goodbye, they *"wept with one another, David weeping the most"* (1 Sam. 20:41 ESV).

When Jonathan saves David's life, he knowingly gave up his own future for David. David's kingdom and household came at the cost of Jonathan's. I think that is why David wept the most when they parted. He knew the sacrifice his friend was making for him. He knew his future would be void of this miraculous, kindred-spirit friendship with God's love at the center.

When I lost Anabel, I felt like I had lost the Jonathan to my David.

David was shattered by Jonathan's death: *"O my dear brother Jonathan, I'm crushed by your death. Your friendship was a miracle wonder, love far exceeding anything I've known-or ever hope to know."* (2 Sam. 1:26 MSG). Even though David knew he was God's anointed to be king, perhaps he hoped deep down that there would be a way to keep Jonathan as a part of his life. It was a devastating loss to his soul.

You never forget the ones your soul loved most. You never replace a true kindred spirit. When a human soul bares itself completely to another human soul, the Lord is in their midst. And when one soul passes on, the left-behind soul never forgets the miracle of their bond. Come kingdom or victory or family or prosperity, the left-behind soul never ceases to ache for the soul it lost. The picture of the future will never be complete.

Years later, David has everything: a kingdom, a family, and a future, yet his heart still aches for Jonathan. So, he seeks out a way to honor his love for Jonathan. In 2 Samuel 9, David discovers that Jonathan's son,

Mephibosheth, is still living, and he commands for the young man to be brought before him.

Can you picture when David sees Mephibosheth for the first time? Searching his face for traces of his beloved friend. His heartbreak at seeing the fear in this crippled young man's eyes. And to banish away all fears, David claims him as family. Just as David, the humble shepherd boy, once sat at the king's table with his future king and forever friend, Jonathan, now Mephibosheth, the crippled and disgraced prince in hiding, is welcomed as family at King David's table.

Grief may mellow over time from fresh and raw into quiet and seasoned. But the soul never forgets. All these years later, my heart still aches for Anabel. I long for her wisdom, I miss her laugh, and I miss the incredible joy and comfort I found in her sweet friendship. I wish she could meet my family now. If I had a kingdom, I would happily give it in exchange to have my dear friend back in my life. The shock of her passing has eased over time into a steady, constant longing in my heart. Anabel's friendship changed my life forever, as did the loss of that friendship. But I will forever be in awe at the sweet miracle and wonder of having such a precious friend.

THE LONELY
IN-BETWEENS

WHEN I THINK OF THE ARRIVAL OF SPRING, I think of the 1993 film adaptation of *The Secret Garden*: flowers blooming out of the melting snow, baby animals learning to walk, and an angelic choir singing in the background.

Not so with Lubbock, Texas.

The transition from winter to spring in Lubbock is not a pretty one. You can be getting sunburned in shorts and a t-shirt one day, and the next day you are bundled up in five layers, driving to work in sleet and ice. On the days in between those two extremes, it just blows unending amounts of dirt. If you have never been to Lubbock, you might think I am exaggerating. But seriously, I cannot emphasize "unending" enough. On those days, the sky turns brown, and my most frequently used piece of vocabulary is "UGH." Honestly, the in-between days can sometimes be worse than the extremes.

In many ways, my grief has been like Lubbock weather in the spring.

I may wake up on a random Tuesday morning with an open spirit, seeing the beauty in the world and feeling a desire to smile and maybe even laugh some. I think about who I have lost without a trace of bitterness, sweetly surrounded by the grace it was to have had them in my life.

And then, I may wake up the next morning with an unbearably heavy heart. It does not matter how good the day before might have been. I can't define it or explain it, but life feels helplessly dim, and the only thing I can manage to do is weep.

And then, there are those lonely in-betweens.

The lonely in-betweens are the days that turn into weeks that turn into months. Not the milestones, not the anniversaries, just time steadily passing by.

When you wake up on an in-between day, you can find yourself thinking that you would take pretty much anything—the cold, the heat, the hard, the good—over having to go through another brown-skied, lonely day. Without question, anyone's first choice would be a good day, but at least on the hard days, others know to come and walk alongside us.

The lonely in-betweens are an unending stream of ins and outs: in and out of bed, in and out of work, in and out of the store, in and out of appointments, in and out of meals. And while you work your way through the daily drudge of ins and outs, your heart and mind are far, far away.

And these brown-sky days start to feel terribly lonely because deep down, you begin to wonder if you are the only one with a heart and mind far, far away. When you are always thinking about the things that no one seems to talk about anymore, far, far away feels farther and farther away, and the lonely in-betweens start to look hopelessly long. Will true spring ever come? Or will it always be this never-ending pattern of ups and downs filled in the middle with desolate, windy, dusty, gritty, in-between days?

I have a couple of things to say today about the lonely in-betweens.

First, I have to offer my most heartfelt gratitude for the ones in my life who have come alongside me in the windblown, hair-stuck-in-your-chapstick, grit-in-your-teeth, lonely, in-between days. On the days when my mind and heart feel miles away, the thoughtful kindness of these people renews my balance between treasuring the hope that lies far, far away and cherishing sweet moments in the here and now.

There are the ones who have followed the promptings in their hearts on random days to check in to let me know they remember and they care. Those precious, sweet surprises serve as a wind block, a brief reprieve from the howling winds and brown skies, and they send smiles and sunshine straight into my heart.

And then there are the small handful of people who have come down and lived in the dust storm bunkers with me, bearing the grime of daily grief with astounding grace and compassion. It takes my breath away and fills my heart with awe to receive the hands and feet of Christ like that.

Second, I want to tell you what happens every year in Lubbock. As winter fades into spring and spring blooms into summer, the dust storms occur less and less. The sun shines more and more. The birds begin to sing their songs again. The days fill with light and grow longer. The grass turns green (or as green as possible in West Texas) and each year, hope begins to bloom in my heart as I watch the seasons change.

Why the hope? Because if the seasons never fail to come, then the One who created them must be just as faithful.

That truth gives me the hope I need to grit my teeth (literally) and face the hot, the cold, and the barrage of wind and dirt I have ahead in my grief. I may have quite a few of the lonely in-betweens left to travel, but I believe with all my heart that there is a new season coming—a season of unbridled, uncontainable joy.

"...As surely as the sun rises, he will appear; he will come to us like the winter rains, like the spring rains that water the earth" (Hos. 6:3b).

"Even in darkness light dawns for the upright, for those who are gracious and compassionate and righteous" (Ps. 112:4).

Perspective

On November 24, 2015, my dog ran away.

We were getting ready to leave town for Thanksgiving, so we left the door from the kitchen to the garage open as we loaded the car for our trip. Darcy usually stays close by, so we didn't worry as he wandered in and out of the garage and the driveway. We were almost finished packing the car when I looked up and realized that Darcy was nowhere in sight. I called his name a few times and walked to the corner of our street to see if I could spot him. Nothing. My stomach dropped. We lived just a couple of blocks away from a very busy intersection. If he made it that far, his chances were not good. I frantically called to Heath, and we dropped everything to begin our search.

Heath did that loud whistle thing I have never been able to do, and I was calling Darcy's name over and over again. My breathing was rapid and my eyes were filling with panicked tears. What if we couldn't find him? Finally, Heath spotted Darcy a few streets down in our neighborhood. He had taken our normal walk route without us, and he had no idea what all the fuss was about. My heart rate slowed down as I wrapped my arms tightly around my dog. All I could think was, "What a horrible Thanksgiving that would have been. I'm so glad everything turned out okay." We dropped Darcy off to stay with Heath's parents and began our Thanksgiving travels.

Later that same night, my sister died in a car accident.

That really changes the way my story looks, doesn't it?

I have entered a new season of perspective. In all my life, I have never experienced a time where the world seemed so full of hateful, deafening noise as there is right now. And in all my life, I have never had a time when I so desperately needed peaceful silence to flood my heart.

While everyone on my social media spent their time screaming out their opinions about the election, I was wishing I could be given the time for a sweet, simple conversation with my sister. I would love to tell Lauren that Blue Bell ice cream was back, that the new trailer for *Beauty and the Beast* was out and it looked amazing, or that I may or may not have bought a new pair of shoes and I was definitely not sorry about it. When all around me was the roaring commotion of deadlines, stress, pressure, and expectations of daily life, all I craved were my sister's quiet words of wisdom. Through the horrible noise of 2016, my heart quietly whispered, "This world doesn't matter. This won't last. I know what truly matters."

The petty drama, the senseless violence—I saw it all through different eyes, my new eyes. Grief shoves many unexpected things into your life: fear, confusion, hopelessness, fatigue, and anxiety, but it also provides clarity. I'm not clever enough to come up with a better name for it, so I call it "grief goggles." The things in life which irritate my eyes and cloud my vision are now held at a distance so I can see clearly. I still see those things and encounter them, but my grief goggles give me the perspective I need to see the difference between temporary and eternal.

When we lost Darcy, I could not imagine a worse way to spend Thanksgiving. But that was before the unimaginable happened. I wish with all my heart that November 24, 2015 had never happened, but I would never wish away the perspective that specific moment will give me each day for the rest of my life. I have plenty of days where I let the muddy water seep back inside of my goggles, and I lose my perspective in those moments. But I have too many pieces of my heart waiting for me in heaven to ever let me completely forget that perspective.

In 2016, I talked less and thought more. I hurried less and cherished more. I desired this world less than ever, and I longed for heaven more than words could describe.

My prayer for 2017 is that I will grow in that perspective. I want to become intentional about creating space for my heart and soul. Space for silence. Space for depth. Space for truth. Space to be filled with God, my Savior, and His Spirit, so I may see Him more clearly each and every day.

"One thing I ask from the LORD, this only do I seek: that I may dwell in the house of the LORD all the days of my life, to gaze on the beauty of the LORD and to seek him in his temple" (Ps. 27:4).

Cusco and Cuy

THIS IS THE STORY ABOUT THE TIME I WENT to Peru and cried over my cuy.

Heath and I were given the amazing opportunity to take a mission trip to Peru this year. I'd never had the chance to travel outside of the country before, and I just happened to be married to my own personal Spanish translator, so I was full of anticipation for our adventure.

But everywhere I looked in Peru, everything we did, I just kept thinking about Lauren.

When we found out we were going to be staying in Cusco, I thought about Lauren. I thought about all the Emperor's New Groove jokes she and I would make in our conversations about this trip.

I kept thinking about Lauren on the long, international flights and as I nervously went through customs for the first time. Lauren never got the chance to take a trip out of the country, but we had quite a list of places we dreamed of seeing someday.

I thought about Lauren as I wandered through the marketplace, picking out souvenirs. I wished I was on the hunt for a beautiful, blue, Peruvian scarf to take home to my beautiful, blue-eyed sister.

As we rode trains and buses through the beautiful mountains, I thought about Lauren. I wondered if there are mountains in heaven like the ones I was currently witnessing in Peru; I thought maybe her healthy, strong, heavenly body would let her explore those divine heights without ever growing weary.

And then, I thought about Lauren when I ate cuy.

Cuy (pronounced coo-ie) is a very special meal in Peru. Cuy is what they cook on birthdays and for honored guests. Cuy is guinea pig.

So yes, I cried when I ate guinea pig. But not because I am a city girl; it actually wasn't that bad if you didn't look at the pen outside with the dozens of live guinea pigs who were saved for another meal. I cried because of the beautiful people in Huancalle, Peru who cooked the guinea pig for me.

We were invited to share a meal at the house of the preacher of the church in the mountain town of Huancalle. When we pulled up, the preacher, his wife, their daughters, and his brother and his wife all came spilling out the door to greet us. We were ushered into a room where they made sure we all had seats at the table before they would sit down. The women ate in the kitchen and spent their time making sure the plates in front of us stayed full. Next thing I knew, they were pulling up another chair at the table and had invited our van driver to join us at our meal. Everyone was invited to participate in this joyful feast.

They stood together as a family and sang in their native tongue, Quechua, to welcome us. Their songs were songs of praise to God, and tears of joy streamed down the preacher's face while he sang. Then, we ate and ate and ate.

Then came the tears. One by one, they stood in front of us to speak, sharing their hearts with us as we finished our meal. Every single one of them was moved to tears as they spoke of the goodness of the Lord and of their love for us, their brothers and sisters they had just met. They told us they would hold us in their prayers, and I believed them. They told us we were always welcome at their table, and I believed them.

They pulled us in. They welcomed us, they sang to us, they fed us, and they served us. They instantly loved us because of Whose we were, not because they knew anything about us or had much of anything in common with us. The one thing we had in common was the only thing we truly needed.

I was moved and humbled by the heartfelt words and tears from the gentlemen, but it was not until the women spoke that I could not stop the tears that began streaming down my face. They stood before us, looked us in the eyes, and claimed us as family. The older women talked about how their own family members, their siblings, were not believers, so we, the body of Christ—we, the ones sitting at their table and eating their food—were the only family they had. And I thought of Lauren, and my heart broke with these women.

I don't use the word "sister" very lightly anymore. In fact, I hardly use it at all. Not with the sweet girls from my social club in college, not even with my best and dearest of friends. That is a sacred word to me now, a word that only truly applies to one person, one role in my life that can only be claimed by a beautiful, long-brown-haired, sparkling-blue-eyed soul in heaven. But as these women looked me in the eyes and claimed me as their sister, I felt my heart making that claim right back to them. For reasons beyond our control, our earthly, biological families were not what they should be, but God brought us together across oceans and mountains to show us that we are not alone. We have family in each other. And I could not be more honored to call those women my sisters.

As we departed, we embraced, and I quietly wondered if I would ever see these newfound sisters of mine again. And then, like a burst of flame, hope leapt up inside of me because I remembered a deep, steadfast truth about my life. Because of Christ Jesus, I have family in Peru who loves me, and in the same way, because of Christ Jesus, I know I *will* see that family again. Hallelujah!

But you had better believe if I am ever privileged enough to travel back to Peru, I will be finding my way back to the little mountain town of Huancalle so I can cry over my cuy with my sisters again.

"For this reason, since the day we heard about you, we have not stopped praying for you" (Col. 1:9a).

My Favorite Stories

When I'm in the middle of a good book, I cannot stand to put it down. Just one more page, just one more. I want to know what happens next. I want to stay with the story. When I have to put it down, I walk away thinking about it. Those are the best kinds of books.

But not all of the best stories end happily ever after here in this world. The greatest stories, the ones that need most to be told, are the ones that are vibrant and deep and good, no matter how short they may be, or whether they pan out the way you expected them to or not. These are the kind of stories that when they end, you walk away with something changed down to your very core, and you long to be better in every way.

I have seen far too many beautiful stories get cut short in my lifetime. It is a shocking, off-balance sort of feeling. Your mind is jarred to a halt and says, "Wait, what? This can't be the end." Your heart immediately mourns and yearns for just one more day, just one more.

In the quieter moments of your grief, you wonder about what could have happened next. You think about how the world would have been different if their stories had gotten to continue. You wish more than anything you could keep reading this beautiful, unique story you loved so dearly. You feel like you ended the last chapter on a cliffhanger and there is no way to read the next chapter to resolve it. Things feel so terribly unfinished, and that feeling is so terribly unsettling.

Not all of the best stories get their happily ever after here in this world, but the end of a story in this world is far from the true end of a story. There is a new heaven and a new earth, and an eternity of all the best stories unfolding into the greatest story ever told.

WHAT SHE GAVE

I REMEMBER THE DAY ANABEL TOLD ME SHE quit the swim team. We discussed it, rumbling down the road in her huge white truck. I was very surprised at first; swim meets and dark-thirty morning workouts were a large part of Anabel's life. "My coach wasn't going to let me go on trips with the youth group anymore," she explained as she maneuvered through traffic. She told me that it had become very clear to her that there was no way swimming should be more important to her than her church family. Anabel had concluded that relationships built at church would have more significance for her life in the long run. "Besides," she told me matter-of-factly, "now I'll have more free time to do things for other people." *That is how she always spent her time: doing things for other people.*

...

"Here you go," Anabel told me, handing me a heavy paper bag. She had received multiple sacks full of clothing, barely-worn, from a friend. "These are too cute for me, and you'll look good in them." *Clothes she didn't need became an opportunity to bestow a blessing.*

...

I marveled as I watched her move confidently through her kitchen. I'd never had the kitchen to myself to cook a whole meal, but when Anabel said I could help her make dinner for our friends, I figured I would be capable of pitching in. But she had everything prepared long before we got there. She sent the boys outside to figure out how to grill steaks, while she and I warmed everything else up inside. We took our completed dinner outside and ate on a picnic table next to the house. The breeze picked up, coming in from the fields on their farm, but we didn't care. We all held our heads a little higher that night, because we had successfully played adult and cooked dinner by ourselves without help. *Now, I think that a boost of pride and confidence were the real gift of the evening, not food.*

...

She leaned forward in anticipation as I opened her present—a sparkling silver orb hung on a black leather cord. She was clearly excited, yet still slightly unsure. "Do you like it? Are you sure?" Then she sheepishly admitted that there was a story behind picking it out. Accessory shopping wasn't Anabel's strong suit, but making conversation was. That's why she had had no qualms approaching a complete stranger in the store to ask, "Is this cute?" when picking out my necklace. We all roared when we heard the story. Anabel flashed a smile and shrugged, "The lady said she liked it, so I figured it was good." *The true beauty of the gift was the heart and effort that went into picking the right thing.*

...

"Flowers would brighten the day of your close friend." The paper slip from the fortune cookie was taped to the outside of the dark green plastic flowerpot packed with potting soil and budding red flowers. *Just another day with just another gift to say, "I love you."*

...

I could tell he was uncomfortable. I'm sure part of his manly pride was smarting to admit that he'd never driven stick shift before, but the other part was mortified even further to learn in front of his friends. But Anabel insisted that there was no time like the present to learn how to drive a stick, and she vowed to teach him. We all piled into the tiny car, three of us crammed in the back, and two in front. Finally, after several lurching laps around the block and through the neighborhood, she decided there had been enough lessons for the night. I sat quietly in the backseat, thanking my lucky stars that Anabel hadn't thought to ask me if I knew how to drive stick shift. *Postponed plans and patient instruction combined to make a memorable gift of time.*

...

The journal was decorated with green, patterned scrapbook paper. Green is my favorite color. She had pasted the letters of my name across the front that bubbled up from the still slightly-wet glue. Inside the journal was a letter explaining the gift. For forty-two days, the number of days between thinking of the idea and my birthday, Anabel had written a favorite scripture on each page. Beneath each verse were her own thoughts. Her letter said it was to make up for the Bible study we had always planned to have together. *She gave me the gift of always being able to study with her and hearing her insights into scripture.*

...

I shuffled to my locker through the drudge of another miserable school day. That year had not been a good one for me, and each day at school was about finishing quickly so that I could go home. I opened my locker to put away my books and found a little cardboard box inside. The box was labeled "Peace O' Cake" and through the plastic window I could see a beautiful cupcake piled high with green and pink frosting. A sheer yellow ribbon held a tag that read, "I love you and so does God! Hope this helps your day go well! Love, Anabel." *Sweet surprises were one of the primary forms of her love language.*

···

I stared at the check in my hands, and Anabel's words echoed through my head: "If I ever won the lottery, I'd split it with you so that we could both pay for college." Her parents didn't know about that conversation, but they had decided that the little that was left of Anabel's college fund should still go to someone's school expenses. It wasn't much; it might pay for a couple of semesters' worth of books. *To me, though, it was a fulfilled promise.*

···

Anabel never stopped giving: trinkets, time, things she no longer needed, and things that were a sacrifice to lose. She gave wisdom and insight, laughter and new experiences. Most of all, she gave her own heart wholly to whatever she did. I am better, the world is better, because of what she gave.

BIRTHDAYS
IN HEAVEN

DEAR LAUREN,

I've been giving this a lot of thought, and I really think
they must celebrate birthdays in heaven.

Each and every soul in creation has been thought of,
loved, and knit together long before the light of the sun
ever touched our faces or we filled our lungs with our
first breath of air. How could such intentional design
and care come to a halt simply because one passes from
temporal into eternal? No, we were designed for eternity from the very beginning. I believe we will fully
experience the unending Love who created our inmost
being. And in eternity, there is infinite time to celebrate every piece of God's infinite creation, from the
countless stars and galaxies he breathed into existence
to each dusty soul into which he breathed life.

You, Lauren, were fearfully and wonderfully made. In
the presence of your Creator, your soul has come into

its fullness, into the richness of its complete and perfect design, into the beauty of its fulfilled purpose.

Today, I believe heaven celebrates all the things that make you especially and uniquely you: your heart of compassion; your radiant smile; your passion for that which is good, pure, and lovely; and your tender care for God's creation. All of these things and more make up the beautiful fabric of your soul—and heaven can't help but celebrate and rejoice over these things about you because they reflect the glory of your Creator.

So, happy birthday, sweet sister of mine. We celebrate you here, and I long with eager anticipation for our heavenly celebration.

All my love,
Lindsey

Mary and Martha
(A Gentle Spirit)

Two sisters, two very different sides of the same coin. Strongest when together.

Leading up to the accident, mine and Lauren's lives seemed to be running parallel to each other. Heath and I started dating in December 2010; Lauren and Trent began dating in January 2011. Lauren and I both went to LCU. We had different majors, but most of the same extra-curricular activities: choir, social club, Honors courses... Lauren graduated in May 2013, got engaged the next week, and we threw a winter wonderland wedding in December 2013. I got engaged a few months later, and we threw a Christmas wedding in December 2014. 2015 rolled around, and Heath and I both graduated from college.

Our life events were back to back, so close together they were almost happening one on top of the other. Lauren and I were learning the ropes together of how to be wives and all the silly, good, and very hard things that came with our new season of marriage.

November 2015 arrived, and we were headed into a more peaceful, joyful, restful holiday season than we'd had as a family in years. Our destination was Abilene, and then down to South Texas all together. All of us were driving on Texas highways that night in the dark. Lauren and I were both riding in our little Toyota Corollas with our newlywed husbands. And there, the parallels and connections were severed. I made it to Abilene, and Lauren did not.

In the aftermath of the accident, all of those similarities frightened me a little. Why was it her and not me? Why did I have to be the one left behind with a shattered heart? Why did I get more time with my husband? What if the next holiday season had me following in her footsteps yet again? Morbid, I know, but anxiety consumed me.

As news of Lauren's passing spread, people poured forth their words and thoughts about her. One phrase emerged over and over: "gentle spirit." And it is 100% true about Lauren. I've never known anyone more fiercely compassionate and empathetic, and her gentleness was immediately evident to all.

One day, my anxious thoughts were swirling around in my mind, hounding me with all the "what ifs" — what if it had been me? What if it still happened to me? What would people say about me? All of a sudden, a thought broke through and popped the bubble of my anxious thoughts. It caught me so off guard that I laughed out loud.

There is no way on earth that anyone will use the words "gentle spirit" to describe me after I'm gone.

I would laugh them right out of my funeral if they tried. (Which is probably the perfect example of why those words would be a poor description of me.) Then another thought followed and surprised me again: that didn't bother me.

I don't have to be Lauren. Our lives may have run parallel to each other, and we were practically identical in the areas that mattered most. But outside of those areas, we could not have been more different. Lauren was the alto to my soprano, the woodwind to my brass, the whisper to my shout. She was quiet but hated being alone, while I am loud and love nothing more than alone time. I love honey and she hated it. She liked tomatoes and I have never been able to make myself eat them. We were two beautifully unique sides to one coin. Lauren was the Mary to my Martha.

I think the world needs both Marys and Marthas. God created us both, didn't he?

I head to bed around 9 pm most nights so I can spend my days tackling to-do lists and making things happen. I love to put my time and energy into doing things or making things for the people I cherish. Lauren, on the other hand, would stay up all night just to talk to the ones she loved, and then she would sleep the next day away accomplishing nothing else. The quality time was more than worth the cost of productivity to her.

When I go back and read through my old texts with Lauren, they are full of me reminding her what time we needed to be somewhere and her sending me pictures of little things her students made for her...typical Martha and Mary, right? Without a doubt, on this side of things, I wish I had sometimes been a little less punctual and practical. Every Martha could use a few more Mary-like qualities, but that doesn't mean it is bad to be a Martha. I'm convinced that Marys and Marthas are actually at their best when they have the other to compliment and contrast them. The harmonies sopranos and altos create together are far more beautiful than either one would be on their own. Lauren may have been late to everything, and I may have a bad habit of running right past things that don't move fast enough, but between the two of us, you found a happy medium of quality time and gift giving/acts of service. Our strengths balanced out each other's flaws.

So, yes, I'm fairly certain no one will ever remember me for my "gentle spirit," but they don't need to. Hopefully they will remember the fresh loaf of home-made bread I gave them on their birthday, or the hand-written note I sent them just because. Maybe they'll remember the way I made them smile or made them feel loved and important. Because those are my Martha strengths.

I miss the Mary side of my coin every day. I feel like my Martha weaknesses are exposed and a little too prominent without Lauren. I still try to imitate some of her quiet, intentional Mary habits, and I truly do want to be more like her in so many ways. But if there's one thing I know about my Mary, it is that she loved me for so many of the things that made me her Martha. So, when the "what ifs" and the anxieties crowd into my heart and mind, I will think about Lauren's gentle spirit and focus on being the best version of me that I can be for however long I may have on this earth.

CALL ME MARA

MY MIDDLE NAME, CAROLINE, MEANS "SONG of Joy." Maybe it is because I come from a family of musicians, but I have always liked that meaning. It sounds poetic and dreamy and prophetic.

Think about the simple songs of joy that pop up in everyday life: getting a letter in the mail (yes, the real mail); the first time you pull up on a wakeboard without falling face-first into the water; taking a bite of fresh-out-of-the-oven homemade bread; hearing someone say "I love you" for the first time; laughing, talking, and eating around a table with family and friends. These little songs of joy well up inside of you. They add seasoning to your life—a sweetness, a richness, a fullness, a saltiness, a zang, and a zest. When you taste a song of joy, every fiber of your being soaks it in, savors it, and sends back the report: this is special. This is good.

Anabel and Lauren were two of my greatest songs of joy, two of my favorite songs to sing. They brought out the meaning of my name in me more than just about anyone else.

When I was with Anabel, I *felt joyful*. With Anabel, I tried new things and was not afraid. I saw the world through different eyes—I saw its bigness and fullness, and with Anabel, I dared to dream about changing it. Anabel gave me the joyful fullness and freedom found in a rare, kindred-spirit friendship. With her, I felt more, thought more, and laughed more than I ever have. She made me brave, she made me compassionate, and she made me joyful.

When I was with Lauren, I not only felt joy, I wanted to *bring joy*. During the dark, gray days that she battled chronic illness, I would come home from school and make a complete fool of myself to bring some sunshine to her days. I ruined a lot of peaceful family pictures because I could make Lauren laugh like no one else. I would keep a running commentary to make her laugh, and her giggles would only make me behave worse. My poor mother could never get a serious picture from the two of us. Lauren was my partner in crime, and if you have ever had one, you know the thrilling joy that comradery gives. Lauren was the soft, silky saxophone to my loud and proud trombone...together we made jazz so joyful you could not help but dance when you heard it.

The seasons of life that carry those songs of joy are sacredly sweet. But when those songs of joy get cut short, life suddenly tastes very bitter. When I lost Anabel and then Lauren, my songs of joy were lost with them. I did not fit my name anymore. I no longer knew how to sing.

Naomi lost her songs of joy too. She and her family left their home because of famine. Then, her husband died, followed by one son and then the other. No home. No husband. No children. No hope for the future. Just a couple of sweet daughters-in-law. After convincing one to go home and being unable to shake the other one, Naomi picks up and travels back to her homeland.

The people back home recognized her and called her by name: "It's Naomi!" But Naomi no longer fit the meaning of her own name. No longer Naomi, no longer "pleasant," no longer joyful. *"Call me Mara,"* she says (Ruth 1:20). Not pleasant, but bitter. Not full, but empty. I used to think Naomi was being a little insensitive to Ruth, who had left her home and family to be with Naomi, but now, I imagine Ruth was feeling pretty empty herself. Two women with no hope for the future, two women who have nothing left to do but cling to each other and drink from the bitter cup that has been handed to them. No songs of joy in that household.

But God steps in, as he always does, and brings beauty out of the brokenness and redemption out of the hopelessness. Through Boaz, God provides a new, little song of joy: Obed. Obed brings smiles to a mother and grandmother who thought they could never smile again. He brings the promise of a future when it seemed there was no future left to be had. While he doesn't replace those who were lost, Obed brings a little fullness and sweetness back into Ruth and Naomi's empty and bitter lives.

I cannot help but think that as Naomi held baby Obed, her heart wished she could have seen her own sons become fathers. I am sure she ached to share the joy of being a grandparent with her husband. But those bitter longings were now mixed with the sweet bundle of joy she held in her lap. Naomi's song was no longer the carefree, pleasant song it once was, nor was it the empty, bitter, despairing silence it had become. Instead, Naomi's song was deep and rich and bittersweet—a combination of heartbreak and celebration—a song whose every note rang of God's goodness and faithfulness. If you ask me, that bittersweet song sounds a lot like hope.

I am still learning how to sing again, learning how to fit my name again. But that is the thing about joy, isn't it? Joy surprises you and wells up inside of you. Some days you feel quite certain that you will never sing again, and then some days, you find that you can't NOT sing. My songs of joy may always hold a hint of bittersweet while I am here on this earth, but I am holding out in hope for when I finally go home. The sweetness of reunion, the praise-inspiring holiness, and the undeniable *goodness* of it all are sure to produce the most glorious song of joy you have ever heard.

THIS IS IT

SEPTEMBER 1ST NEVER MEANT A THING TO me. It came and went every year, and I passed by it without a second thought. But then I married a hunter. Apparently the first of September is a HUGE DEAL. It is the first day of dove season, which might as well be a national holiday in our house. Who knew?

Last week, I got some valuable insight into this sacred, blessed day. We woke up on the morning of September 1st, and before we were even out of bed, Heath began having a very serious conversation with our dog, Darcy. It went a little something like this: "Darcy, do you know what today is? September 1st. This is the day you were *made* for. We are going hunting tonight, and you are going to fetch so. many. birds. This is your *purpose* in life."

Now, there are two kinds of people who are reading this right now. Half of you (I like to call you "Team Lindsey") are cracking up at how ridiculous this all sounds. The other half of you (let's call you "Team Heath") simply do not understand why this story could possibly be considered funny. You think everything Heath said to Darcy makes complete sense.

I lay there listening to Heath's pep talk and just rolled my eyes and laughed. He can try to brainwash that dog all he wants, but we all know Darcy's true purpose in life is to be a big, fat mama's boy. Not surprisingly, Heath came home from hunting that night to report that Darcy (suddenly *my* dumb dog) had only fetched one bird and chose to spend the rest of the hunt relaxing in the shade of a tree. I have never been more proud of my baby. I trained him so well.

Here's what I learned, though: September 1st is a day of purpose, a day intended for a man and creation. It is the kind of day where people on Team Heath open their eyes in the morning and cannot go back to sleep because it is a special, precious, rare day.

You don't have to be a hunter to have those kinds of days. You know the ones I am talking about—those days in your life when you wake up and your first thought is, "This is it. This is the day." Immediately, you are wide awake and can think of nothing else. The first day of school was always like that for me, as was the last day of school. Sometimes those mornings happen on the day you are scheduled to leave on an eagerly-anticipated trip, and sometimes they come in the form of a hard-earned graduation day. The morning of my wedding was like that; I woke up and thought to myself, "This is it. This is the day I become a wife."

But these kinds of days are not always joyful or exciting. They come in the form of heartbreak too. They come the day after you have lost someone: "This is it. This is my first day without this person." They come on the days of funerals and burials: "This is it. This is the day I say goodbye to my spouse, my child, my sibling, my friend." They come on test result days and on court dates. They come on anniversaries and birthdays, and they come on regular days, too. "This is it. This is my life now."

When you have lost someone, "this is it" echoes through your mind, resonates through your heart, and buries itself deep down in your soul, never to leave. This is it. *This is it.* But slowly, if you let it, "this is it" begins to take on new meaning. When you carry such a fresh, firsthand knowledge of the fleeting preciousness of life, the rare gift of each day dawns in your heart each morning. "I did not have to wake up today. Some people did not wake up today. This is it; if I am here, today must be a day of purpose for me. I am a human, designed to participate in creation. I am not here by accident; I have work to do." Grief awards those who carry it a special perspective on the priceless value of each day.

I miss many things about my pre-grief life, but I do not miss my pre-grief perspective. The hope of heaven becomes dearer and dearer to me each day, and I become increasingly homesick for heaven with each precious person I watch go on before me. As time marches onward, busyness and stress crowd in around my heart, but each day, my heart now whispers, "There must be more than this. I know what truly matters."

In grief, some days you wake up and it feels like August 31st...just a day you have to get through to make it to the next day. Hear me when I say that there is absolutely *nothing* wrong with that. But today, I want to challenge you to start looking at your days like they are September 1st. When you wake up and think, "This is it," try adding on to the end of that sentence. "This is it: today may feel like just another day, but today is the day I was *made* for. What is my purpose today?" Sometimes all it takes is a little Team Heath pep talk in the mornings. When you practice an attitude of anticipation, even in the midst of great sorrow, your grief and loss will never be meaningless.

I believe with all my heart that when my time comes and I finally find myself in heaven, my overjoyed soul will breathe a sigh of relief and say, "THIS is it!"

Grieving with Hope

Lauren's favorite poem was by Emily Dickinson. And this poem is *so* Lauren because it is all about hope.

The first stanza says:

> *"Hope is the thing with feathers*
> *That perches in the soul,*
> *And sings the tune without the words,*
> *And never stops at all"*
> (Dickinson 1896).

I love those words because they were special to Lauren. But I don't always soak them in fully. The past two years have had their fair share of moments that felt pretty hopeless for my soul. And I sometimes begin to wonder if that little thing with feathers has flown away to perch somewhere else.

1 Thessalonians 4 talks about how believers do not grieve as those who have no hope, which sounds really

nice on paper, but my heart thinks very differently sometimes.

We may not grieve as those who have no hope, but oh, sweet friends, do we still grieve!

This paradox of grieving with hope, this bittersweet journey (sometimes feeling awfully overloaded on the bitter side of things) has me turned all sorts of upside down. What does grieving with hope even look like? I'm no expert, but here is what it has looked like to me over the past two years:

Grieving with hope looks like getting out of bed each day.

Grieving with hope looks like letting the built-up anguish of your heart spill out through your heavy tears—and then settling into a quiet, subdued peace because you know your cries were heard.

Grieving with hope looks like the constant battle between heart and mind: what you feel to be true versus what you know to be true.

Grieving with hope looks like giving thanks for the relief of lighter, happier days, and it looks like giving thanks for the sustenance and strength to survive the darker, heavier days.

Grieving with hope looks like finding a way to smile about the sweet memories even as you weep over the bitter ones.

Grieving with hope looks like accepting the limitations of what your hurting heart can handle and seeking out help when you become overwhelmed.

Grieving with hope looks like finding a way to reach out and hold the hand of another broken heart. Not every broken heart in the world, mind you (remember: accepting limitations) but the ones the Spirit tugs you toward. Because your grieving heart understands their hurt just a little better than most.

Grieving with hope looks like showing up. Showing up to weddings and showers and holidays and birthday parties and church and school and work. Showing up to life—despite the fierce, silent ache in your heart.

Grieving with hope is just what it says it is.

Grieving: allowing yourself to feel the depths of the sorrow of your broken, anguished heart. Refusing to feel guilty over what you should or shouldn't be thinking, feeling, or handling from moment to moment. Taking each storm of emotions as they come—anger, despair, doubt, weariness, loneliness—and riding out the waves without trying to avoid them.

Hope: clinging to the knowledge that your broken heart, this broken world, is only temporary. Refusing to feel guilty when better, brighter days roll through and you allow yourself to enjoy them. Knowing that God loves to give good gifts to his children, and you have not been condemned to endure a lifetime of despair and sorrow before you can enter the joy of eternity. Hope, because each tear you cry brings you one drop closer to no more tears. Hope, because each day you complete brings you one day closer to an eternity of light.

So, weep. Laugh. Grieve. Hope.

The feast is coming. God himself will tenderly wipe away the last of the tears. His holy, radiant light will forever cast away the shadow that death throws over our lives.

Invite that hope to perch in your soul and sing its sweet song. You'll start to learn the words if you let it sing long enough.

Still Here

Dear Lauren,

Things are changing around here. I knew this season would come, but the shift has still caught me off guard. I've had no peace for weeks, and rest has been elusive. Finally, I went to bat for you in my dreams last night. You and I were together, and people you knew and loved were saying goodbye to you and moving on with their lives. You were quiet and didn't say much, but I could see and feel your hurt. In that moment, I was no longer just your little sister; I went full on mama bear. I stepped in front of you and put you protectively behind me to shield you from any more hurt. These people were not getting through me to you.

I don't remember my exact words (there were many) but I remember a few very specific sentences. "How dare you? How can you act like she isn't here? She's standing right here. She's still here!"

She's still here.

When I woke up, I couldn't get those words out of my mind. The wordless grief that was weighing me down in my waking hours became clear in those three simple words from my dreams: she's still here. As the world continues to march onward, deep in my heart of hearts, you are still here. Your role in my life has not changed and will never change. You are still my one and only sister.

Very few people have room in their hearts and lives to keep someone else's grief at the forefront of their minds all the time. Everyone means well, but to set up camp in the valley of grief is hard and uncomfortable. It wasn't their loss, it is not their burden. There are new people to pray for, new crises to command their attention. Our tragedy becomes old news at some point. But in my world, your loss will always be earth-shattering news.

All these years later, I still dream that everything was just a big misunderstanding and you are alive and well. And I know you truly are alive and well (much better than well, in fact) with God. But as long as I draw breath on this earth, you will always be alive here too, with me.

The world may move on, but I will forever stay with you. You're still here.

All my love,
Lindsey

THERE IS HOPE

I SAW THE MOST BEAUTIFUL THING LAST WEEK.

I was driving along when I spotted a funeral procession approaching me. My heart always lurches when I see a funeral procession because I've been there. I remember the shock and the numbing sorrow. I remember the hopelessness as you face the end of what you assumed your life would look like. All these things and more flashed through my mind when I saw that long row of blinking lights on the cars. I remember.

And then I saw it.

Over on the side of the road, a group of rough and tough construction workers stopped what they were doing, removed their hard hats, and stood at attention for the procession.

I wanted to weep and rejoice all at the same time when I saw the kindness of those construction workers. I wish I could have rolled down my window and thanked them—thanked them for halting their daily grind to recognize that someone else's world had come grinding to a halt that day. There isn't really much anyone can do to ease the pain of a day like that, but those men took their hats in their grimy hands and offered their respect and their compassion.

I haven't been able to get that image out of my head. As I drove away, it struck me that those men probably looked a lot like Jesus' disciples when they encountered the widow of Nain. In Luke 7, it tells us that Jesus and his disciples were going to the village of Nain when they encountered a funeral procession leaving the town. I can just see the disciples, covered in dirt and grime from their travel, stepping aside and bowing their heads in respect.

The scripture notes that the deceased was the only son of a widow. The grieving mother had already lost her husband, and now her son too. She had no one left to provide for her. She was facing the end of what her life should have looked like. This procession was a parade of hopelessness. A long line of people blinking away tears.

Have you been there? Have you sat under those tents in a cemetery? Have you stared down at that green, turfy carpet a few feet away from a casket and had your vision blurry with tears? Have you taken part in one of those hopeless days? I have.

Yet in the midst of loss and sorrow, when the rest of the world doesn't know what to do except step aside, Jesus steps in.

He doesn't shy away from the raw devastation of grief. Instead, the man of sorrows overflows with compassion (Luke 7:13) when he sees our aching hearts. When Jesus saw the widow of Nain, hopeless and futureless, he stepped in to provide for her. As much as I wish he would step in and halt all of our funeral processions, I cannot deny that he has stepped in and tenderly provided for my needs.

When death has me feeling defeated, Jesus sends me sweet reminders that he has defeated death. When I think that death has robbed me of my future, Jesus steps in and restores it to me through a beautiful, quiet morning or a warm ray of sunshine. When I lose hope that this world has forgotten how to love, Jesus shows me a crew of construction workers stopping to pay their respects to a person and a family they will never meet.

There is hope.

BLUE SKIES

SOMETIMES I THINK I BELIEVE IN GOD'S goodness the way I believe in the sky being blue: an overarching, out-of-reach fact to be seen and known only from a distance.

But yesterday was one of those days where the vast, West Texas sky was so vibrantly blue I felt like I could reach out my hand and touch it. And if I touched it, I knew it would pull me in and I would be forever falling, tumbling through its deep, blue richness.

As I looked up at that endless stretch of sky just inches from my face, I didn't just vaguely know about the goodness of God the way I halfway remember a story I read once...I could *feel* it. All-encompassing, all-consuming—filling my lungs with each breath I took, pushing each little gust of breeze that played with my hair, bursting out of each little bird I heard chirp and chatter, and soaking through each drop of warm sunlight. The simple beauty of his goodness took my breath away, and before I knew it, that goodness had pulled me in and tumbled me around where all I could do was marvel at its deep richness.

My circumstances had not changed. I did not receive back the ones I have lost. The things that keep me awake with worry and pump stress through my veins were still there, patiently waiting off to the side for me to remember them. But all I could think as I stared at that stunningly blue sky was, "I lack nothing."

That's the first time I've thought those words in over two years.

Then the words of the Psalmist floated through my mind: "*The LORD is my Shepherd, I lack nothing...*" (Ps. 23:1). I lack nothing. In fact, I have an excess. I have so many sweet blessings in my life, but I could lose them all and I would still lack nothing because of God's deep, unending goodness.

His goodness gives us green pastures for restoration and quenches our souls with the water of life. His goodness guides us through the mountains and valleys, even the valleys covered by death's shadow; it brings comfort to our hearts and gives us reason for joyful feasting—no matter the circumstances. His goodness calls us and gives us purpose. Our days are filled with his goodness and mercy, and each day his goodness brings us closer to home.

Our skies won't always look blue. Sometimes God's goodness seems to be more of an intellectual fact in our minds than a tangible experience in our hearts. But yesterday reminded me to reach out and touch the sky—to taste and see the Lord's goodness.

His goodness satisfies the soul as with the richest of foods. Yesterday, I caught a taste and a glimpse of it from a beautiful, blue sky. Where will you find it tomorrow?

"Oh, taste and see that the LORD is good! Blessed is the man who takes refuge in him!"
(Ps. 34:8 ESV).

BIG CHANGES

DEAR LAUREN,

You aren't going to believe this, but it looks like we are probably moving to Colorado. I wish so desperately that I could talk to you. The first thing I would say is how very sorry I am for not visiting you more when you moved away. I knew you were lonely, and I tried to check in often, but as your sister, I feel like I should have done so much more.

I am so terrified at the thought of leaving everything and everyone I know and love. How did you do it? How did you give up your job and life and comfort like that? I know it tore you apart, but you still did it. You did it for the love of your husband and for the future of your family. You're the bravest person I know. I'm so sorry you never got to have your future family.

I am so afraid that my move away from Lubbock will be like yours. I wish you were here to walk me through it. I wish you were here to give me advice on how to support my husband when I don't feel like it. And I wish you were here to come see me before I move. I remember the day you moved. We went to the mall with Mama to do a little shopping. Out in front of Bath and Body Works, we took those silly pictures that I love so much. I really didn't want you to leave, and I know you didn't want to either. I remember saying goodbye with a lump in my throat thinking things would never be the same again. I had no idea how right I would be about that.

I miss you like crazy. I hope you find a way to come see me in Colorado.

All my love,
Lindsey

Planting Seeds

We got the call to move from Texas to Colorado just two days after we had planted our garden.

I was so sad to leave for so many reasons: our families, our friends, my job, our house…but for some reason the thing that made me cry was our garden. I kept thinking through every part we had all planned out: all those tiny, little seeds we planted with such expectations; the paint swatches I picked up when we bought the seeds, thinking we might repaint the exterior of our house over the summer; missing watching those sweet, little, green buds push their way through the sandy soil and dead pine needles; the flowers that would bloom and then slowly wilt away into baby vegetables; the fresh squash casserole I would cook to share around our table with the loveliest people; and the sunflowers that would climb up the south wall of our house. We were going to miss it all.

I have this dreamy, nostalgic thing about sunflowers. When I was little, my parents would plant what felt like countless rows of jumbo sunflowers in the backyard that grew as high as our fence. In reality, there probably weren't as many as I thought, and they probably weren't even that tall, but to me and my sister, they were a green and golden forest to explore. Lauren and I would put on our Pocahontas dresses and discover the New World, singing about the colors of the wind. I remember even when the glory of the sunflowers had passed, their faces would become heavy with mesmerizing spirals of seeds—a harvest for the next year.

So, out of all the things my heart was mourning at the thought of moving, the garden seemed to represent them all. The memories we wouldn't get to make in that house. The plans and dreams we had to set aside for this new, unexpected calling. And, oh, those sweet sunflowers. What a loss.

And as I thought about all those seeds we planted, I started to think about my dear friend, Anabel. Anabel came from a family of farmers. She knew plenty about growing a garden. But her expertise was in the seeds she planted in people's hearts. Seeds of boundless love. Seeds of unbridled joy. Seeds of laughter, hope, and determination. The garden in Anabel's own heart produced a bountiful harvest of the fruits of the Spirit. From that fruit, Anabel took seeds to plant and invest in other's lives. And I had the extraordinary honor of being one of her many gardens. I followed alongside her, learning how to plant, nurture, and grow heart-gardens in others.

I remember my first thought when I heard the news of Anabel's passing: "But she wasn't done here." She had so much left to do. So many more seeds to sow. So many more lives to change. She couldn't possibly be gone. Look at the harvest the Lord produced through her in her short years here; think of the harvest he could produce through her in a full lifetime.

And yet, even as I remember those first feelings of grief, it strikes me that Anabel was never concerned with the harvest. That was in the Lord's hands. Anabel's concern was with being obedient to her calling. Planting the seeds she was called to plant. Letting the fruit of the Spirit in her life spill over into the lives of those around her. And years later, the seeds she planted while she was here on earth are still growing, producing, and multiplying far beyond what any of us could possibly imagine.

The harvest is out of our hands. Our calling is simply to plant seeds everywhere we go, as long as we have breath.

That realization gave me the peace I needed to let go of my little, un-sprouted garden and look for my calling in a new season of seed planting.

*"See, I am doing a new thing! Now it springs up;
do you not perceive it? I am making a way in
the wilderness and streams in the wasteland"*
(Isa. 43:19).

TINY MIRACLES

IN THE LAST CHAPTER, I TOLD YOU ABOUT how I grieved over my garden when we found out we were moving. I mourned leaving those seeds behind just like I mourned having to leave our sweet house that felt more like a home in the six months we lived there than any other place we had ever lived. I felt a little silly, but I knew I was really mourning the loss of our plans and dreams.

But God is so very sweet.

In the final few weeks before we moved, the sunflowers I had lovingly planted along the south wall of our house began to grow like weeds. They strained and stretched and reached for the sun. I could almost see new, little leaves unfurling out of the corner of my eye, and I could swear they sprouted two more inches every time I turned away.

About two weeks before the move, Heath told me to go look in the backyard. There, standing tall and proud, was the most perfect, little sunflower I had ever seen. My heart burst with joy. What a sweet, precious gift!

My world wouldn't have ended without that sunflower. It didn't change the fact that we were leaving everything we knew behind. But in the midst of God asking us to do this big, scary thing, he knew that my heart was sad over my flowers. He didn't have to do anything about it, but he did.

The overwhelming sweetness of his gift took my breath away, and here is why:

For years, I have wrestled with how to pray. Too many instances of heartbreak followed by deepest grief have made me afraid to pray boldly. I pray for the things I can be certain of—I beg God for his peace, his faithfulness, his comfort—but I never pray for miracles. Not anymore. Because miracles don't seem to happen for me. The answer has always been no. And sometimes I don't know how much more disappointment and grief my heart, or my faith, could take.

A few months ago, I was talking to my counselor about my struggles with prayer, and she pointed me to Matthew 7:9-11: *"Which of you, if your son asks for bread, will give him a stone? Or if he asks for a fish, will give him a snake? If you, then, though you are evil, know how to give good gifts to your children, how much more will your Father in heaven give good gifts to those who ask him!"*

That concept has echoed through my heart, mind, and prayers ever since—*God loves to give good gifts to his children.*

More often than not, your answer could very well still be no. Your job may still be miserable. Your diagnosis may still be grim. Your path may still be hidden. The world around you may still seem to be falling apart. But we know that all of the ugly brokenness Satan throws our way could never even cast a tiny shadow over the glorious goodness of God. So, even when the answer is no, there is always hope because God is always good.

And yes, God works in the big picture—a bigger, grander, more perfect, big picture than we could ever imagine. But I want to tell you today that God also works in the tiniest details. When you open your heart and your eyes, God's good gifts and tiny miracles are everywhere. Something as small and insignificant as a sunflower that says, "I AM working. I AM sovereign. And I hear your heart." With all the big-picture life changes swirling around me, that sweet, little sunflower became the good gift my heart needed. In that moment, that tiny miracle was as big as the world to me because I felt seen and heard and loved.

We said goodbye to that house in the dark, early hours of the morning. But I took my husband's hand and led him outside to our backyard before we left. The sky was inky black, and the neighborhood around us was silent. My miracle sunflowers (with two or three more blooms by then) slept soundly, heads bowed, nodding and swaying, waiting for the sun to rise. A handful of stars sprinkled the sky, and a tiny, little crescent moon shone down on us. I took a deep breath, said a silent farewell to my sleeping sunflowers, and walked away. Closing a door, starting a new chapter.

As I followed the moving truck out of town, I stared up at that sliver of a crescent moon and the empty outline of where the rest of it would grow to be. And I heard a whisper in my heart, "Watch me fill you up."

I'm learning to believe in miracles again. A sunflower and a crescent moon, my tiny, little miracles, are teaching me to keep my eyes open. What good gifts. What a good Father.

Driving Me Nuts

Dear Lauren,

I dreamed last night that you and I went to the Grand Canyon. I was so annoyed because you said you wanted to sleep in until noon before we went to the canyon. I kept trying to tell you that it would be way too hot and way too crowded if we waited that long to go, but you were determined.

I love that dream because it was like nothing changed. Like you never left. You were taking your sweet time, and I was getting impatient. Both of us, two extremes, with the common ground of sisterhood to pull us together. A modern-day Mary and Martha.

I miss you. I miss our perfectly imperfect relationship. I miss all the things about you that drove me nuts. How you would sleep through your alarm for what felt like hours when all I wanted in the mornings was peace and quiet. How you left your crazy-long hair spread all over the bathtub. How you sometimes wanted to be goofy and silly when I didn't want to. How you packed so. many. bags. for just one little trip. How you always wanted to play your latest mix of songs on road trips, and how you had long, mushy-gushy phone calls with Trent in the car where all the rest of us had no choice but to sit and listen.

I miss the quirky little things about you that I always thought were weird. How you always used three towels after a shower. How you stuck your finger in the inside of your lip to get it wet when you wanted to clean the mascara off your eyes instead of just licking your finger. And speaking of mascara, how you couldn't ever apply it without your eyes looking like a sleep-deprived raccoon's. How it didn't matter how many times I showed you how to do your eyeshadow, you still never knew how to do it. I never minded doing it for you, but it still made me laugh. How you munched on jumbo-sized Cheez-Its in the car until just the smell of them could make me sick. (I tried some again just the other day thinking they couldn't be that bad. I was wrong.) How you applied lotion with one finger. How you always requested cherry cream slushes from Sonic but couldn't ever finish them. How you had your little routine anytime you got in the car to drive: pull your glasses case out of your Vera Bradley purse; put on glasses; pop the case back shut with a loud click; check all your mirrors; put the car in reverse; check and adjust your mirrors again; slowly begin to back out. It took forever. You were kind of a granny driver.

Now, I'm sure if you were to read this letter on my side of heaven, you would be more than a little irritated with me. I'm sure you have an even longer list of my annoying and weird traits. But I'm hoping the bigger picture of heaven helps you see my heart behind these words. I don't want to forget one single thing you did that got under my skin. I miss <u>all</u> of you, Lauren. Your flaws, your perfections, your quirks. I would give anything to have you back, even on the days you absolutely drive me nuts. That's what sisters are for, right? To fight and squabble and pick and poke and play and laugh and cry and laugh-until-you-cry and defend and protect and share and listen and talk and exchange glances behind your parents' backs and celebrate and dream and hope and encourage and love beyond anything imaginable.

That what sisters are for, and you, dear sister, were the best of the best in all of those categories.

All my love,
Lindsey

FOGGY MORNINGS

I DROVE TO WORK IN A THICK FOG THIS morning. I left the house long before the sun was up, and the inky black of leftover night swirled in between the earth-bound clouds. I couldn't see a thing around me—no buildings, no landmarks, just the beam of my headlights on the road right in front of me. As I drove the still new and unfamiliar route, keeping my eyes glued to the tiny patch of light ahead of me, I let my mind drift to all the things I can't see, all the things I don't understand right now.

See, my heart is wrapped in a thick fog this morning too. The year has slipped into yet another fall season. I can't seem to stop them from coming. All the dates, the reminders, and the string of cold, cloudy days that make my heart ache. Last night was one of those nights I cried myself to sleep. Years later, they still come.

I write a lot about blue skies and sunshine and tiny flowers that breathe glimpses of hope into my weary heart, but some days the clouds don't roll back to reveal blue skies. The air is too cold for blooming flowers.

And the heavy grief clings to my heart the way the fog has clung to the ground today. I can't see. I can't understand. I can't possibly understand how I'm going to get where I'm headed, wherever that is, because I can barely see my next step right in front of me.

On days like today, you can try to remember the blue skies and the past promises fulfilled. But sometimes the fog rolls in so tightly around you that it starts to cloud your memory. Sunshine and flowers seem to be distant promises from another time and another life so far away you might have dreamed them. They can't touch or break through the fog you face today.

How do you make it through the foggy days when you can't see, you can't remember, and you don't know what to do? I wish I knew. The only thing I can do today is just to keep putting one foot in front of the other.

In the Shadow of the Mountains

We have lived in Colorado for a little over four months now, and I've gone and fallen in love with the mountains. I'm not entirely sure how it happened; I've always been a wide-open-spaces kind of girl, but the mountains have drawn me in and enthralled me.

The mountains look different every single day. Some days they are smooth and picturesque like a watercolor picture on a postcard. Some days they look so sharp and clear it takes my breath away. I feel like I'm looking at a high-definition TV screen because that view can't possibly be real. On cloudy days, I watch the wispy clouds slip and roll over the peaks like a waterfall. On rainy days, the blankets of water blend in with the mountains in patches of blue, gray, and purple like a cozy quilt. There are days when the forest fires get out of control, and the mountains look hazy like a mirage. Last month, the first snowfall of the year dusted the tips of the peaks in white powder that they will wear throughout the whole winter season.

The mountains are infinite layers of texture, both scraggly and smooth: rocky faces hiding soft, flower-filled meadows; rough and rugged pine trees mixed with the slender and graceful aspens; roaring, tumbling rivers and still, quiet lakes. But in the evenings when the sun is going down, all those details flatten out into solid, monochromatic layers of indigo peaks—never ending, fading from dark to light into the sunset like dozens of paper triangles all lined up and overlapping.

I love the mountains. When I'm driving around, trying to find my way through the maze of this city, I can always look up, spot the mountains, and know I'm not completely lost. When I'm caught in daily mundane tasks like unloading groceries into my trunk at the store or sitting through traffic, I can look over and have my breath taken away all over again by the glory of the mountains that watch over my daily life. Everywhere I go, I feel like I see a new angle, a new facet of the mountains. I keep thinking I've seen it all, that I've found the best viewpoint, but then I round a corner, and WOW! A new perspective of the splendor hits me, and I find myself speechless all over again.

Some days I wake up and the clouds, smoke, fog, or rain have rolled in so thickly around us that I can't see the mountains at all. No matter how hard I look or search—I can't see them or feel them or sense them in any way. Those days make it easy to feel lost or directionless. That steady, unfailing presence suddenly feels removed, and I'm left feeling a little off-balance.

But here's the beautiful part. Even though my head knows I can't see the mountains that day, my heart subconsciously makes me keep looking for them. They have become such a part of my daily life, that I can't imagine my little world here without them. It doesn't make any sense to keep searching for something you can't see, but I know deep down, without a doubt, that those mountains are still there. That they will always be there, even when I have no hope of seeing them.

So, when I turn a corner that has always held a beautiful view before, my instinct is to look up for the mountains, even on the gloomiest of cloudy days. Every once in a while, the clouds will part just long enough for me to catch a glimpse before they close back up. In those moments, no matter how brief, my heart says, "Ah, there you are." And that tiny glimpse is enough to make me keep searching, keep waiting and looking day after day. Without fail, no matter how long the clouds choose to stay, I always eventually wake up to blue skies, sunshine, and a spectacular view of the mountains.

I'm sure you see where I'm headed with this. God is teaching me so much about himself during this season of living in the shadow of the mountains.

God is mighty and spectacular. To seek his face every day is to live a lifetime of learning new things. In him, you will find the rushing thrill of a call to new and unknown kingdom work. In him, you will also find the quiet, still peace of his healing rest and love. Every time you think you have God figured out, he will give you a new perspective and transform you all over again. God is infinitely, intricately detailed, but he is also eternally and unchangingly One—the Way, the Truth, the Life, the Word—I AM WHO I AM.

There will be days in your life when you see God more clearly than you ever thought possible. You will taste his love, you will breathe in his presence, and he will seem so close you feel as though you could reach out your hand and touch him. I try to remember to savor and celebrate those days. Drink them in and let him weave his presence deeply into your heart; seek his face as part of your daily routine. Because the days will roll in where you will wake up, and no matter how hard you look, you will not be able to see him. The fires will be on their path of destruction. The chaos of a crisis or a tragedy will cloud your view. Or the fog of complacency may have simply rolled into your life when you weren't looking. And all of a sudden, you can't see him anymore. You are lost, you are directionless, you are hurting, bewildered, and broken.

But, dear heart, he is there.

You may not see him, hear him, or understand him, but he still sees, hears, and understands you. He is steadfast. He is unfailing. He is working, even when you are blind to it. So, let your heart keep searching. The world will say it makes no sense to keep looking for something you can't see. But I promise you without a doubt that he is still there. It doesn't matter what you can or can't see because HE STILL IS. Life storms and circumstances may be able to come in and cloud your vision, but they couldn't possibly remove a mountain.

And when the storms pass and the clouds are rolled back, you will once more behold the radiant glory of God—immovable, steadfast, and relentless in his love for you. And your heart will smile and whisper, "There you are."

"I lift up my eyes to the mountains—where does my help come from? My help comes from the LORD, the Maker of heaven and earth. He will not let your foot slip—he who watches over you will not slumber; indeed, he who watches over Israel will

neither slumber nor sleep. The LORD watches over you—the LORD is your shade at your right hand; the sun will not harm you by day, nor the moon by night. The LORD will keep you from all harm—he will watch over your life; the LORD will watch over your coming both now and forevermore" (Ps. 121).

Big News

Dear Lauren,

You're going to be an aunt! I can hardly believe it. The doctor said it is way too early to tell anyone, but you already know, so I can tell you all about it. I wish I could describe the awe I feel over this tiny, little miracle growing inside me. I feel like Mary—"How can this be?"

Oh, how I wish you were here to do this with me. But I promise to keep writing and tell you all about it. I hope the baby is a girl so I can name her after you—to carry on your beautiful spirit. I hate that my babies won't have their Aunt Lauren here at their birthdays and recitals, but I know you are loving on this little bundle of joy right now—getting ready to send him or her to me with all your love.

I have no idea how I'm going to do this. I'm terrified and overjoyed. I'm so afraid of losing this baby—in the womb, in life, or in faith. Since the day I first thought I might be pregnant, my prayer has been that I will honor

God and do right by this baby every day I get to be with him or her. With all that I am, I want this baby to grow to love the Lord. If they give their heart and life to God, we will handle whatever else will come our way.

As always, I wish you were here.

All my love,
Lindsey

Twenty-Six

Dear Lauren,

Last week I turned twenty-six. And I can't get you out of my mind. I haven't counted the exact days—I don't want to know—but in a few short weeks, my time on this earth will have officially surpassed yours.

So much about our lives as we turned twenty-six looks similar: living hours away from all family; spending most of our time at home alone as the husband gets settled in his new, important job; being members at a new church with only one or two new friends; trying so very hard to make a strange place feel like home.

I wish I had understood more of what you were feeling then as I do now. Of course, I missed you when you moved, but I was still surrounded by all my friends and all things comfortable and familiar. Now, lonely and so very far from home, I wish had gotten to come visit you more than once—spent some time in Artesia cheering you up, seeing your new world, and making you feel missed, remembered, and valued.

Yet, as much as our lives mirrored each other, they also feel solemnly different.

As I look back at newly twenty-six-year-old Lauren, I see how your life was drawing to a rapid, unexpected close. And at twenty-six myself now, I have a husband of over four years, a baby on the way, and countless journals, scraps of paper, and documents filled with letters to you and words about life and death, despair and hope, grief and joy. I've never written so much in all my years as I have in the past three-plus sisterless years of my life. I miss you.

Somewhere, in the back of my mind, the "what ifs" creep in. What if my days are to be cut short like yours were? What if I only get a limited amount of time with Heath and this little baby instead of growing old with them? Those thoughts, unhealthy as they may be, make me set my mindless phone aside. They make me sit down and write something, play the piano, straighten the clutter in my house, sit outside and turn my face to the sun. Those thoughts make me pursue beauty, peace, and order rather than ugliness and comparison.

As always, you still make me want to be better.

All my love,
Lindsey

Heaven and Earth (Here)

I will be the first to admit that I know nothing of the glories of heaven or how it all works. But ever since I discovered I was expecting a baby, long before I knew her name or even that she was going to be a girl, I have had this image that I have not been able to get out of my mind. Whether it's true or not, I have felt these whispers and glimpses of heaven and earth as the drops of comfort and strength for which my heart thirsts. Besides, miracles happen. I know, because there's one growing inside of me right now.

"Here," he said as he cupped your hands together and placed it carefully in your grasp. "I want you to be the one to hold this precious soul. I am fearfully and wonderfully knitting the body together right now. Your sister is preparing to love and raise her on earth, and when the time is just right, we will send this soul with all the glory of heaven right down to unite with that miraculous, growing, little body. Until then, I want you to be the one to hold the soul of this precious little image-bearer."

"Here," he whispered as he touched my womb. "Here is where she will form and grow. I want you to be the one who raises this precious child. Your sister is in heaven, taking the tenderest, sweetest care of her little soul—singing to her, telling her stories, loving her with all her heart. And when this little girl comes to you, she will bring along my glory, my promises, and my image, wrapped in a sweet, joyful bundle of love. Have courage, dear one. Victory is mine."

Here, now, he is weaving her together. He is carefully writing her story. He already knows every single day of her life—what she will do, who she will become—just as he already knows every single hair on her head and every freckle on her nose. His work in her will be wonderful; I know it well, and I believe it fully.

Here, now, you see the whole breathtaking picture and all of our roles in it. You whisper to me that this grand, unfolding story will be the greatest ever told. In just a few, short weeks, that radiant, rare, and precious soul will fly from your loving arms to mine. And I will see a little glimpse of the pure joy of heaven. I will get a little taste of your sweet love once more here on earth.

"For you created my inmost being; you knit me together in my mother's womb. I praise you because I am fearfully and wonderfully made; your works are wonderful, I know that full well"
(Ps. 139:13-14).

SINGING TREES

I MAY NOT KNOW WHY GOD HAS PLACED US here, or what our future holds. But today, right now, in this moment—it is enough for my heart to know that I live in the Land of the Singing Trees.

Back home, the to-do list is growing faster than I could ever hope to catch it. The laundry is piling up, and I couldn't tell you the last time I dusted. Brakes need replacing, and insurance isn't covering what it should. Things we were promised are being pulled out from under us, and bank accounts are uncomfortably low. Friends and family are all hours away, and the back pain won't let up. I've been overwhelmed, despairing, even.

But here. Now.

The trees are singing and it stills my soul. The birds chirp to each other, and the wildflowers bounce and sway in the sunshine. The wind weaves its way down the mountainside, tickling the tops of the trees in its path. If I sit still and listen, I can hear the song winding its way toward me. And then with a joyful burst, it hits the trees surrounding me. They erupt into song, leaves dancing and boughs swaying to the music. Then, as quickly as it came, the song fades to a whisper yet again as it travels on down the mountain to other eagerly waiting tree tops and listening ears.

This wind song that the trees and birds and flowers love so dearly to sing has a way of rushing and swirling down to quiet my very soul. It teases the wisps of hair around my face and sweeps away the fears and anxieties weighing down my heart. Then, oh, my unburdened soul flies to the tops of the trees to dance and sing with the birds and the leaves. Together, we send the praise-filled songs of creation on down the mountain and out into the earth—wherever the wind will carry it. And there is peace in my soul because I know that he is God, and I am not.

"Be still, and know that I am God" (Ps. 46:10a).

Victory

I'VE BEEN MISSING YOU FOR FOUR YEARS now, Lauren.

I stare at my daughter, your niece, and I think about how she is everything I prayed for. I would have fiercely loved any baby, but my heart so desperately wanted a girl so I could name her for you, catch a glimpse of you in the squint of her smiling eyes or in the color of her hair in the light.

I cried on the way to the appointment where we would find out what our baby would be. I felt like I knew deep down that she was a girl, but I didn't want to be disappointed if the baby turned out to be a boy. But the minute I saw her, before I even knew her gender, I was in love. When they told us she was a girl, my heart knew immediately that she was my Laurel. For the entire hour-long ultrasound, I watched her little hands and feet move around, and I wept at the holy beauty of it all.

Every time I pause to look at this little, living miracle with each of her tiny, perfect features, my heart is broken open and filled with light by this precious gift. Yet at the same time, I feel the terrible weight of what I lost in you perhaps heavier than ever.

I lost getting to see you hold my brand-new baby girl at the hospital. I lost your hands-on love, prayers, and involvement in Laurel's life as she grows up. And some days, it feels like losing you all over again.

We named this girl for you, Lauren, "Laurel-Crowned." Your names mean Victory—a word I claim over your life, mine, and hers. Death does not get the victory in our story. Our victory rests in the hands of the Creator of Life—life to the full and life everlasting.

I hold this little bundle of victory in my arms, and I proclaim that God is good. Not simply because something went right and I feel blessed, but because he was also good when things went as wrong as they possibly ever could. He is as good through the 3 am feedings as he was when I was up at 3 am weeping at the nightmare of grief from which there is no awakening. We get to stand among the broken pieces of our hearts and of this world and shout victory because the goodness of God is unshakable.

Little Laurel, my glimpse of victory, is both the lightening and the deepening of my grief. She simultaneously softens and sharpens the ache of missing you. I hope she sees you in me and that I see you in her. Together, our three souls celebrate the life that was, the life that is, and the life that will come. And may the Creator of our souls be glorified through it all.

Star-Filled Skies and Soft, Sleepy Sighs

I'VE MADE THIS TRIP MORE TIMES THAN I can count in my lifetime. Holidays, summer vacations, weekend visits. I have such vivid memories of traveling this road with my family as a child. Long hours in the car listening to Celtic Woman cds or Hank the Cowdog books on tape. But some of my favorite moments were when we traveled at night. My mom and my sister would fall asleep. My dad drove with quiet confidence because he knew the road like the back of his hand. I felt safe and secure.

Always, I turned my gaze to the night sky outside my window. Brimming with countless stars, it drew me in deeper and deeper. As I stared, I imagined big, great things for my life—travels, adventures, love, and magic. Anything felt possible. I felt an irresistible tug drawing me toward the unknown to see what marvelous discoveries awaited me there. In these silent moments, I felt all the vastness and the wonder of the universe, and the greatness, holiness, and beauty of it all stirred my soul.

For the past four years, travel has been a source of deepest angst and heartache for me. It dredges up all the fear and grief and broken memories of how we lost my sister. Travel in the dark holds a particular terror for me. The wide, endless highways now hold horrors, not wonders. I stare straight ahead at the road, trying so hard to shut out the images that tend to pop into my mind. And honestly, in some ways, I think it will always be that way for me. But on this trip, for the first time in a long time, something felt different.

Once again in our lives, we find ourselves facing the unknown. Once again, we step forward with trembling hearts and blind faith. As we travel in the dark, early hours of the morning, in the driver's seat is my husband, now a father himself, leading his family with his quiet, steady strength. I am riding in the backseat next to our sleeping baby, sitting in the same spot I called mine for all our family trips. Staring out the window, I feel the wonder stir up in my heart again. The same wonder I felt as a child.

I stare at my baby girl fast asleep, and I marvel that the One who created the grandest glories of the universe also crafted each impossibly long eyelash, invented the unique color of the blush on her cheeks, and designed the sweetest little hands and feet in the world just for her. I stare up into the vast, glittering sky, and the longer I watch, the more stars begin to appear as my vision adjusts to their splendor. Each one like a promise slowly being revealed as our path carries us ever forward.

I don't know where this road is leading, but I have confidence in the One who guides the journey, and I anticipate the final destination. As stripes on miles of pavement speed toward us and disappear behind us, anything feels possible in this moment of vast unknowns stretching beyond our sight. I look to my right and see an endless, West Texas sky glistening with stars; I look to my left at my precious, sleeping daughter. I am surrounded by star-filled skies and soft, sleepy sighs, and I know in my heart the One who holds our lives in his hands.

Laurel's Aunt

Dear Lauren,

My heart aches with missing you this morning. I think I was already feeling anxious because I had a nightmare last night, and then Heath told me the latest in politics this morning, which stressed me out even further. Then, he made a comment to Laurel about seeing all her aunts, uncles, and cousins next weekend, and my heart just shattered. I know he didn't mean it—he apologized later and said he realized what he'd said the minute it was out of his mouth. But it is so painfully obvious to me that you are missing from the equation of our lives.

All is happy and well with Heath's family. His siblings are having babies, and everyone he loves is here to surround Laurel, his greatest joy. And I love the Holts dearly. There is no family I would rather have as my in-laws. But I will forever ache for the picture of what my own family should look like. I will forever long to see my sister hold and dote on my daughter, and I will forever wish that I had little nieces and nephews that shared my blood. Yours should be the face little Laurel gets excited to go visit. Yours should be the name at the top of my recent calls list and the text chain using up all the storage on my phone because of all the pictures and videos we keep sending each other. I will never stop wishing you were here. I will miss you at every birthday party, every tee ball game, every piano recital, and <u>every</u> <u>single</u> <u>time</u> the subject of Laurel's aunts/uncles/cousins comes up.

You would be head over heels for this little girl, Lauren. She is pure joy! Her wheels are always turning, and she is already very mischievous. She has the funniest little smirk, the sweetest giggle, and the world's cutest booty. It feels like bragging to send too many pictures or stories to Heath's family, but I know if you were here, I could send every single one to you, and you would be delighted.

We discovered this week that Laurel loves blueberries just like you. (Although, as I write this, she is dropping her blueberries over the side of her high chair one by one and watching them fall.) I wonder all the time what else we will discover that the two of you have in common. Each new discovery will thrill my heart and make you feel near for just a moment.

I love you and miss you always.

All my love,
Lindsey

THE BLONDE ANGEL

LAUREN AND I USED TO GET IN THE SAME
fight every year at Christmastime. My mom had a set
of four stocking holders: a Santa, a Christmas tree, a
blonde angel, and a brunette angel. Seeing as how
Lauren and I both had long brown hair, you would
think we'd be fighting over who got the brunette
angel, but it was the blonde angel that was the source
of tension in our house.

I don't remember why. Maybe we just liked her better
because she had the golden hair we would never have.
Maybe it's because she wore a beautiful white dress
while the brunette angel wore a dark maroon dress.
Maybe (and I think this is most likely) I just wanted her
because Lauren wanted her too. Whatever the reason,
we got in a big argument every year when we pulled
out the Christmas decorations about who would get
the blonde angel as their stocking holder. You know,
the kind of thing sisters fight about.

One year, I ended up with the blonde angel. After
Christmas was over and we took down the decorations,

I put my initials on the bottom of the angel before packing it away to save us the argument I knew we would have again the next year. In all likelihood, I probably just picked the right number between 1 and 10 or drew the long straw, but in my mind, we had proven that the blonde angel was mine once and for all.

The next Christmas, when the argument got started up again, I simply calmly and rationally pointed out my initials on the bottom, and my parents (not realizing the depth of our feelings on the subject or remembering the last year's argument, I suppose) accepted that as proof that the angel was mine.

Lauren. Was. Outraged. In her mind, just because I had the blonde angel the year before did not mean it was mine forever. Furthermore, she thought I had cheated and unfairly put my initials on it, and therefore it should NEVER be mine again due to my trickery.

I don't remember who ended up with the blonde angel that year. Probably Lauren. Her righteous indignation was strong. I still maintain that my actions were completely above-board and that I was just trying to record the truth and save us all a hassle. I think it wasn't long before my mom went and bought new identical, neutral stocking holders, though.

I am the only one carrying our stories now. The other side of all my childhood memories are with Lauren. I saw things from a very specific point of view, and now Lauren is no longer here to correct me (or keep me honest) about how she thinks things actually happened.

One of our favorite stories was from when we were very little. We went fishing and Lauren caught five fish and I caught none. Not to be outdone, I went around telling everyone I caught five fish. I wasn't being deliberately dishonest; I just wanted it to be true so badly that I convinced myself that it was. Lauren was not happy about that one, either, and was quick to set the story straight. In many ways, when Lauren passed away I lost the other half of my childhood.

I was caught off guard by how much of a burden it felt to carry our memories all by myself. I had no idea how lonely it would feel or how sad it would be as certain stories began to blur and there was no one to help me remember them. I always loved that it was just me and my sister in our family until Lauren passed away. My sudden transition into being an only child was devastating to me. Yet there is not much in this world that brings me more joy than to remember all the funny little moments we shared growing up. There is something so incredibly special about the years of memories I have of just me and Lauren. No one can claim the relationship I had with Lauren. The title of sister only belonged to us. Although that makes what I lost completely unique, it also makes what I had infinitely precious.

I thank God all the time for the gift of my sweet sister, and I can't help but smile when I think of all the tiffs, trouble, and fun we shared. She made me who I am today.

I Didn't Know

Dear Lauren,

I had a dream this week that you were here and you told me you were pregnant. I tenderly put my hands on your little belly, and I wept tears of joy over you. I could not stop the tears because being with you and having you share that kind of news was the fulfilment of one of my heart's deepest longings. Then, I woke up, and remembered that you weren't here, and the pregnancy I dreamed about was someone else's news, not yours. And for the millionth time, my heart shattered all over again.

Oh, how I wish I could share this hard and holy season of motherhood with you. What I wouldn't give to hold your precious children in my arms and see your arms wrapped around my own. I didn't know I would miss you so much in this season. I didn't know it would feel like losing you all over again or how noticeable your absence would be when my little family started to grow. I didn't know how much I would grieve over the nieces and nephews I will never have. I didn't know I would sit with tears streaming down my face as I watched my daughter toddling around on an uneventful morning, unaware of who is missing in her life. I didn't know how hard it would be to mail invitations for her first birthday party and not send you one. I didn't know.

In the fresh and early days of this journey, I wept to a counselor that my future children would never know you. Her casual response was, "Yes, but you will tell them about her." I did not go back to that counselor for several reasons, but that was one of them. She invalidated my grief. There is no world in which telling my children about you could ever be an acceptable substitute for having them actually know you. Of course, I will tell them all about you, but that will never make it okay that you are not here yourself. I will never stop longing for what things would have been like if you were here.

I didn't know I would still be dreaming after all this time that everything was just a big misunderstanding and you were back here with me again. I thought I wouldn't be caught off guard as often anymore. I thought things would be at least a little easier after some years had passed. I suppose in some ways they are, but in some ways they are harder. I didn't know.

I miss you with all my heart, Lauren.

All my love,
Lindsey

Bits and Pieces

In the beginning, all I could see were the pieces.

For me, it started with a single moment in time. Letters formed words. Words formed a sentence. And that single devastating sentence was followed by the sound of my heart silently shattering into a million pieces. More pieces than I could ever count.

For months, I couldn't seem to move. There were too many pieces. Pieces everywhere. I felt like one of those cartoon characters who gets steamrolled. So I just laid there in flattened pieces and focused on remembering to breathe in and out. In and out.

Breath by breath. Day by day. Piece by piece. Until one day I discovered I had just enough strength to sit up and look around. Looking at the pieces around me. What a hopeless mess. I couldn't clean it up. I couldn't fix it. The broken pieces were all that was left of me.

My only choice was to gather the pieces. To collect all the fragments of myself. So I spread my shaky arms out wide and tried to hold it all. Like carrying a load of laundry—a sock drops, but when I stoop to pick it up, two shirts fall out the other side of my arms. Pieces slip through the cracks and just keep falling. I tried to hold the jumbled pieces together, but nothing fit the way it used to. *All the king's horses and all the king's men...* One wrong move and everything could come tumbling and crashing down again.

Fragile. Shatter-hazard. Pieces upon pieces.

Like a stack of paper thrown into the air and gathered back together, not a single piece of me is where it used to be.

A song came on the radio at work the other day. One I can't sing with her anymore. I trailed off mid-sentence with my boss as the pieces I usually grip so tightly began slipping out of my grasp. I went and stood in the supply closet and let a few tears slide between the cracks to water the pieces of my heart that lay at my feet. The song ended. I wiped the tears. I picked up the pieces, and I went back and finished giving my report. Day by day. Piece by piece.

Sorting through the pieces of her life. Books, notes, buttons, clothes, music, jewelry, papers, knick-knacks.

The pieces that shaped her life now shapeless without her. Looking at it all, my core trembled like plates shifting in the earth. Cracks spread through the pieces of my heart. Pieces split into more pieces.

How would I possibly decide which of her pieces to keep? My arms were already overflowing with all the broken pieces of me.

Her most treasured pieces were stored, ready and waiting for her, in heaven. The pieces she left here are just temporary. But I still live in this temporary world, so they mean something to me.

I carry a piece of her with me every day. Yes, in my heart, but also physically with me. The color blue. A piece of her jewelry. A shirt or scarf that was hers. Her birthstone, her fingerprint.

I wish I could carry all her pieces, but I can't even seem to manage my own. So, I just hold a little piece here and wear a little piece there. Not enough to keep her here in this world, but enough to keep her with me, here, in this world. Just a piece.

I'm no good at juggling all my misfit pieces. But I'm okay with that. Most days I simply celebrate the fact that I am not still flat on the ground somewhere, just trying to remember to breathe. In and out. But the days

I wake up feeling shattered and flattened all over again are okay too. One day, one piece at a time.

I'm learning to be honest with myself about what my fragile self can handle. I've had to set some important pieces down. But I've learned to cherish and hold dear some other pieces of my life.

I know I won't be in pieces forever. And I know that I will even find some healing and wholeness on this side of heaven. But for today, it's okay that I don't always know what to do with all these bits and pieces.

"The LORD is close to the brokenhearted
and saves those who are crushed in spirit"
(Ps. 34:18).

Patchwork

I last wrote about my bits and pieces. My days of feeling hopelessly shattered beyond repair. But I also told you that I believe there is more to life than sitting surrounded by the bits and pieces of what used to be.

The process of going through Lauren's belongings felt destructive to me. Taking apart what was left of her presence here—what to keep? What to let go? Seeing the pieces of her life get broken down into smaller pieces and then scattered. That's a hard thing for a shattered heart to handle.

So, with one small part of those belongings, I decided to make something instead of taking it apart.

I'm no seamstress. I grunt and chop and hack and cut corners through projects that are way above my skill level. And when the messy, crooked product looks semi-complete, I wash my hands of it in exasperation and walk away wondering why in the world I ever thought I could sew.

But going through Lauren's clothing, I got the crazy idea that I wanted to make a quilt. So, I began setting aside shirts: pale blues, soft grays, deep, rich royal hues, pretty florals and ruffles and lace. Every shirt held a memory. I could point to every piece and remember exactly when she wore it.

Then, I stared at those pieces for days. Days turned into weeks, and weeks turned into months. I put this piece here, and that piece there. I switched those two pieces, and then changed my mind and switched them back. Trying to make order out of chaos. Trying to envision something whole out of something so hopelessly broken.

I began to cut into the pieces. As if they weren't already small enough, I had to pull them apart and make them even smaller. That was a long, hard, never-ending process. My back ached and my neck grew stiff, and everything in me just wanted to quit. How could all these pieces ever become something whole and worthwhile? It was too much work. It was taking too long. I didn't want to put forth the energy I knew it would take to make it happen.

But finally, one day, the breaking down was complete. It was time to begin building back up.

Slowly, as I stitched and ripped apart and stitched again, those bits and pieces began to form a patchwork. The lines weren't completely straight, the seams didn't lie completely flat, but the pieces began to have purpose again.

I had long stretches of time where I put the project away. Times where I had to refill and refresh my heart instead of pouring it out. But the project was always there in the back of my mind. I kept planning and preparing. I mentally pinned and tucked and envisioned what I would do next when the time was right.

Finally, just a few weeks ago, about two years after I began the project, I finished my last stitches on the quilt. I stepped back and looked at my patchwork. It was flawed and imperfect. But it was complete. It was something new, something useful, something rich with history and fresh with purpose. My work was not wasted. The bits and pieces became something whole.

And I got to thinking, maybe life is just cycles of bits and pieces and patchwork.

Isn't that what we believe as Christians? That we are being made new again and again by his mercies each day? I don't want to be the same person I was yesterday or the day before. Maybe this patchwork tapestry in my soul is more fully me than my old "whole" self ever was. He continually weaves my scraps and bits and pieces together to look more like him.

It is a long, grueling process. Most times it feels like it will never end, that I will just be nothing but broken and hopeless bits and pieces forever. But the Artist is faithfully working behind the scenes toward his vision, his plan, and his purpose for me. The difference here between his work and my quilt is that his final product will be completely and wholly perfect. I am being filled with new purpose, becoming exactly who he intends me to be.

In the end, these bits and pieces form together to display all the hard work and frustration it took to make that patchwork. These scraps of devastation weave together in artistic proof of where I have been and where I am going. No longer loose bits and pieces, this patchwork can now wrap its arms around me on the days when I feel like all the pieces are falling apart all over again, and it will remind me that only God can make broken things whole again.

Softly, tenderly, the One who formed me—the One who knit me together before I was born—He takes my bits and pieces and begins to make something new. And as he sorts through my scraps, he also weaves new strands of his own into my tapestry that become the themes which hold my heart together: empathy, deep compassion, perspective...and those strands tug me more heavenward than I've ever felt before.

I am not what I was. I am not yet what I will be. I am becoming. And that is a sacred place to be.

"But forget all that—it is nothing compared to what I am going to do. For I am about to do something new. See, I have already begun! Do you not see it? I will make a pathway through the wilderness. I will create rivers in the dry wasteland" (Isa. 43:18-19 NLT).

Acknowledgements

To Heath, for holding my hand in my grief, for always believing in me when I don't believe in myself, and for making my dreams become reality. This book would not have happened without you.

To my parents, for raising us in a joyful, loving home, and for making home a safe retreat even when we grew up. More than anything, for your incredible example of living a faithful life through every storm.

To Ruth, the world's most insightful reader, for making me a better writer and a better person.

To Kaitlyn, the world's most talented designer, for making this book more beautiful than I could have ever imagined.

To my people, the precious souls who have mourned with me and let me hash out my grief time and time again, for staying behind and remembering with me when the rest of the world moved on.

WORKS CITED

Dickinson, Emily. 1896. "Hope" *Poems: Series I-III, Complete*. Series II.I.VI. Todd, Mabel Loomis, and Higginson, T.W., eds. Duke Classics (Kindle edition) © 2012. ISBN: 9781620110607.

Lewis, Clive Staples. 1952. *Voyage of the Dawn Treader*. HarperCollins e-books: EPub Edition © September 2010. ISBN: 9780061974267.

CPSIA information can be obtained
at www.ICGtesting.com
Printed in the USA
BVHW022009240721
612633BV00038B/1125